How to Write Winning Short Stories

A practical guide to writing stories that win contests and get selected for publication

Nancy Sakaduski

Cat & Mouse Press
A Playful Publisher

Cat & Mouse Press
Lewes, DE 19958
www.catandmousepress.com

Published in 2015
Printed in the United States of America

The meaning of a story has to be embodied in it, has to be made concrete in it. A story is a way to say something that can't be said any other way, and it takes every word in the story to say what the meaning is. You tell a story because a statement would be inadequate. When anybody asks what a story is about, the only proper thing is to tell him to read the story.

–Flannery O'Connor, "Writing Short Stories," *Mystery and Manners*

Cat & Mouse Press
Lewes, DE 19958

ISBN: 978-0-9860597-9-7

For my father

Contents

Acknowledgments

I thank Weldon Burge, Robert A. Day, Ramona DeFelice Long, Laurel Marshfield, Mary-Margaret Pauer, and Sandra Wendel for reviewing the manuscript for this book and providing valuable input.

What Is a "Winning" Short Story?

A good short story is almost always about a moment of profound realization. Or a hint of that. A quiet bomb. There is a record by the American singer Tori Amos called "Little Earthquakes." That's a good metaphor for a short story. Often, a good short story will be a little earthquake.

–Joseph O'Connor, "Advice & Inspiration for Writing Short Stories"

A winning short story may be one that literally wins (a contest), one that wins publication (is accepted by a magazine or anthology), or one that is "winning" in a broader sense: a story that charms readers by engaging, entertaining, and connecting with them. This book is for writers who would like to produce a story that fits any of these categories. It is not intended to cover the full field of fiction writing. There are entire books that address setting, scene, viewpoint, or other elements of writing, as well as many works devoted to grammar and composition.

Let this be a practical little manual of tips, designed to provide accessible, actionable advice to short story writers, particularly beginning or emerging writers, who want to write short stories for adult readers. It focuses primarily on fiction, as that is usually what is meant when one talks about short stories.

What Is a "Winning" Short Story?

Why Short Stories?

> The great pleasure for me in writing short stories is the fierce, elegant challenge. Writing short stories requires Cary Grant, Humphrey Bogart and some help from Gregory Hines. We are the cat burglars of the business: in and out in a relatively short time, quietly dressed (not for us the grand gaudiness of 600 pages and a riff on our favorite kind of breakfast cereal) to accomplish something shocking—and lasting—without throwing around the furniture.
>
> –Amy Bloom, "The 'Fierce, Elegant Challenge' of Story Writing: Amy Bloom on Why Short Is Good"

Humans began telling stories as soon as they developed language. They may even have used sign language before speech was used for communication. And with communication came stories. People used stories to warn others about danger, to procure food and other necessities, and to pass on knowledge. They may not have given these early stories titles, but they passed them on from person to person and generation to generation.

Different groups of people shared various sets of stories (we call them folk tales now) as part of their cultural traditions. These stories were often a shared narrative (the work of more than one author) and evolved over time, as they were passed along, much like an Internet meme goes viral and then may be changed by others. With the invention of written language, people were able to write these stories down, and a new means of storytelling emerged.

Given how important stories are to individuals and cultures, it is no wonder that so many people enjoy writing, telling, listening to, and reading stories. From the moment children understand language (and perhaps even slightly before that) until they are nearly too old to comprehend, human beings love stories. People also enjoy creating and passing on stories, whether they are the stories of their lives, stories about others, or stories from their imaginations.

Today, when the phrase "short stories" is used, for most people it means short fiction. Short stories are ideal for people who like entertainment in small doses. Readers sometimes either don't have the time or can't find the interest to commit to a book. Short stories take just a few minutes to read and can be read on a bus or train, in the car (if you're not driving!), while waiting in a doctor's office or carpool lane, during a lunch break, or just before bed. And for people who have poor memories, being able to read a complete story in a single reading is a big advantage.

Publishing guru Penny Sansevieri has said that "short is the new long," and she is right. Kindle Singles (fiction and nonfiction of five thousand to thirty thousand words in e-book form) was launched by Amazon in 2011 and sold two million titles in fourteen months. Twitter fiction, flash fiction, microfiction, and six-word stories are now making the rounds.

While short forms of writing may be enjoying a comeback, the concept is certainly not new. *Reader's Digest* has published short memoir pieces, jokes, advice, and other little nuggets for ninety years. *Best American Short Stories* is a bestseller every year, indicating strong interest in short fiction. Anthologies are also hot right now—for readers, but also for writers. Several professional writing organizations publish anthologies. These include Sisters in Crime, Mystery Writers of America, and Romance Writers of America. Authors can get together and publish a book of short stories easily through self-publishing. And the addition of a better-known author or two can help sell the entire book.

Some people assume that a short story is just a pared down novel, but that isn't true any more than a single joke is a short version of a stand-up routine. Short stories are an art form of their own. There are some stories, particularly those that require long passages of time or a slow unfolding of the inner lives and motivations of the characters, that simply don't work as short stories.

Extremely complex plots are also not conducive to short forms. This does not mean, however, that short stories can't take on big issues or fundamental themes such as love, death, or why people are so fascinated with Kim Kardashian. The number of scenes (and their length), number of characters, number of points of view, complexity of the plot, length of time covered, and length of descriptions and dialogue are reduced when writing short stories.

Different authors have offered various metaphors to compare short stories to novels. Seán Ó Faoláin has said that a short story is to a novel as a hot air balloon is to a passenger jet. Like a jet, the novel takes a long time to get off the ground, carries a lot of people, and takes them a long distance from where they started. On the other hand, the short story takes off vertically, rises directly to a great height, usually carries only one or two people, and lands not far from where it took off.

Della Galton calls short stories a painting in miniature and says that short stories should have "all the depth and colour that a full size canvas allows" but with no room "for waffle." According to Edith Wharton, one *builds* a novel but *hatches* a short story. Dawn Raffel (author of *Further Adventures in the Restless Universe*) says about the short story, "The story is a sprint in which every step and every breath and every flicker of an eyelash matters; a novel is a marathon, a test of stamina, faith, and will."

Short stories are fun and challenging to write. They contain many of the components of a novel (setting, characters, plot), but those elements must be realized in a short format that forces discipline and economy. Some writers enjoy the focus and the need to get into the action quickly. A short story writer must write concisely and at a faster pace; there is no room for repetition and unnecessary detail. Short stories provide a place to showcase smaller ideas and less complex plots. They allow the writer to create more drama in a shorter span of time.

Alice Munro has said, "I don't really understand a novel. I don't understand where the excitement is supposed to come in a novel, and I do in a story. There's a kind of tension that if I'm getting a story right I can feel right away, and I don't feel that when I try to write a novel. I kind of want a moment that's explosive, and I want everything gathered into that."

With a short story, the writer must telegraph information. There is no room for long explanations, large casts of characters, or sweeping expanses of time. In short stories, it is even more important to use active voice, specific verbs, and descriptive nouns (instead of lots of adverbs and adjectives). Short stories are stories seen up close, in high definition, and most are designed to be read in one sitting.

Short stories can be easier to get published because there are many outlets for short stories, including print or online magazines, contests, and anthologies. Getting stories published establishes you as a professional and helps you build a bio. Publication shows agents, publishers, and reviewers that you are serious. The more publications you have, the more visible you will be, as you get more news coverage, mentions on blogs, and presence in social media. You will gain experience with the publishing process, meet and work with editors, and possibly make connections that will help you get additional publication credits.

Short stories can be resold to magazines, newspapers, anthologies, and film or television producers. If you are willing to self-publish, you can even market your own anthology. Awards and contests can provide another way to bring in money (as well as additional publishing credits). They lend credibility, provide visibility, and help you build a following.

It's no wonder that short stories have become popular again. They are enjoyable and engaging to read and challenging, but gratifying, to write.

Getting Started

The Market

> Writing in a vacuum is really very difficult. So try to have a sense of who it's for.
>
> –Joseph O'Connor, "Joseph O'Connor's Top 10 Tips"

The section on marketing short stories is actually at the end of this book, but I'm putting this introduction here as a reminder that you should consider the market before starting any writing project you expect to publish. If you truly write just for yourself, that is absolutely fine, but if you want to publish your work, you must consider the market, whether submitting to a publisher or publishing the work yourself. "Build it and they will come" may work in the movies, but in real life, companies *never* build anything without considering the market, and neither should you.

Considering the market doesn't just help with selling your project; it also helps with the writing itself. If you have an idea of whom you are writing for, you are more likely to produce a successful story. Some writers actually imagine a person they know, but you might imagine a woman relaxing and reading your story on the beach or a man who loves poetry savoring the metaphors in your story.

James Frey talks about the importance of writing for the reader in his book *How to Write a Damn Good Novel, II*: "If you run a janitorial business, say, you've got to know that people like shiny floors and sparkling porcelain. If you're a divorce lawyer, you've got to know your client not only wants a big settlement and alimony, but also wants his or her ex to suffer. Fiction writing is a service business. Before you sit down to write a damn good novel, you ought to know what your readers want."

The salability of a story is a factor of the outlets available, the number of readers interested in that kind of story, and to some extent, current tastes and preferences. Years ago, "true confessional" stories and westerns were popular. Today, it is much harder to find an outlet for those kinds of stories. Story lengths are also getting shorter, with flash fiction and microfiction taking the place of the lengthy stories that were once popular but are now much harder to place.

Keep in mind that you are part of the marketing package. Even large commercial publishers expect authors to build and sustain a following. Before offering a writer a contract, most now consider whether writers have a website, how many Twitter and Facebook followers they have, and whether they are visible in online groups and forums. That is why many writers start blogs and work on building an author platform that will help them build a fan base for their writing.

Choosing What to Write

> The short story is one of the greatest, most challenging, most infuriating forms of literature. They look so easy! That's the thing about really good short stories. They don't read like they were written. They read like they simply grew on the page.
>
> –Joseph O'Connor, "Advice & Inspiration for Writing Short Stories"

What constitutes a short story depends on whom you ask. Generally speaking, a short story should be a length that can be read at one sitting, and that sitting shouldn't include a sunrise and a sunset. For some folks, twenty thousand words is a short story. Certainly if you go back a hundred years or so, short stories could be quite lengthy. Today, most people think of a short story as ten thousand words or fewer at the high end (seventy-five hundred or eight thousand is often used as an upper guide), with one thousand to five thousand words being the most common length. Anything above eight thousand words or so starts to get categorized as a novella. Anything below one thousand starts to get into the realm of flash fiction.

According to Lee Masterson, microfiction is anything up to one hundred words. "This very abbreviated story is often difficult to write," she says, "and even harder to write well, but the markets for microfiction are becoming increasingly popular in recent times. Publishers love them, as they take up almost no room and don't cost them their budgets. Pay rates are often low, but for so few words, the rate per word averages quite high." The example usually quoted (and often touted as the shortest actual story ever written) is this one, which has been attributed to Ernest Hemingway but is probably apocryphal:

> "For Sale: Baby shoes. Never Worn."

An increasingly common category is flash fiction (one hundred to one thousand words), which is becoming a popular form for magazines. These stories are more plot than character and frequently rely on a twist or punch-line ending.

Short stories may or may not fall into a genre (science fiction, romance, mystery, fantasy). If you plan to write a genre short story, be sure to read the genre. That sounds obvious, but unless you know the conventions of the genre and the expectations of the genre's readers, your story will not find an audience. This is not to say you can't be creative, or even that you can't bend or break rules. Just make sure you know the rules and break them intentionally, in a way that will appeal to readers.

While we're on the topic, it's a good idea to read short stories of any kind—to study their structure and pacing, analyze the plot, and consider what makes the story enjoyable. Read good writers who wrote short stories (Stephen King, O. Henry, John Updike, F. Scott Fitzgerald, and Alice Munro). What makes the story good? Examine, analyze, and compare.

Preparing to Write

> Enthusiasm for writing any story is usually greatest at the beginning. When writing shorter works, you get to feel that energy more often—energy that will often transfer to your other writing projects.
>
> –Ian Martyn, "The Power of the Short Story"

If you want to be serious about writing, start with a good work environment. Although people differ, and some writers seem to be able to work in any sort of setting, most people will get more done if they are in a location where they won't be interrupted. This may be a space that is quiet or one that has consistent background noise such traffic sounds, music without lyrics, or loud coffee-making equipment and the voices of people ordering complex caffeinated beverages.

Make sure your chair is comfortable (but not so comfortable as to encourage dozing) and at a proper height for computer work. Know when you are at your most creative and reserve that time for brainstorming and writing. Other times of day are best spent on research, submission processing, and fact-checking.

Create a working space with easy access to paper, pens, and dictionaries and other references. Have a place to jot down (but put aside for now) any ideas for new stories or projects that pop into your head while working on this project. You will want to try to maintain focus on one project at a time (humans cannot *actually* multitask—what we call multitasking is just rapidly moving back and forth among tasks).

Minimize disruptions. Explain to your family and friends that writing is your *work*. You wouldn't interrupt a brain surgeon during an operation to discuss going out to dinner, who's going to do the laundry, or what happened in the last episode of *The Walking Dead*. You are not "just" writing, you are *writing*. Turn off email and social media notifications. Put your phone on vibrate and answer it only if the call is from the Pulitzer Prize committee. Close game apps. Yes, even the solitaire one.

Have good lighting if you are reading or jotting ideas on paper. Eyestrain is a frequent cause of fatigue, so give your eyes a rest periodically, or at least vary what you are looking at (computer screen, text on paper, distance viewing).

Aristotle said, "A job well begun is half done," and it's one of my favorite quotations. Time spent on preparation nearly always pays off, even (or perhaps especially) if you are the sort of person who likes to wing it. Whether you do a full outline or just jot some notes, you will save yourself time in the end by organizing your project before you begin writing. Some people do extensive outlining and prewriting ("plotters"), while others prefer to write by the seat of their pants ("pantsers"). But even most pantsers give a fair bit of thought to the setting, plot, and characters before beginning to write.

There is no one right way to write. Some people will tell you that you should have the story outlined in advance, perhaps on color-coded index cards or in an expensive software program, organized scene by scene, character backstory by character backstory. Others will tell you that you should simply start your characters on a journey and then stand back and write down what they say and do. I suspect these two groups could also be broken down into people who go on vacations with reams of research, ratings, maps, and itineraries, and those who get in the car and drive. Neither is right, as long as the results are pleasing.

Some people like to write a synopsis of the story before they begin. If you find you cannot summarize the story you want to tell, or the description of the story becomes wordy, it may be a sign that the story you are trying to tell is too complicated for the short story format.

When you're planning your story, you can start anywhere you want. You may have the characters in mind first and then need to come up with challenges to throw their way. Or you may have created a perfect climax for a story and now need to set up plot points that lead up to it.

Sometimes the genre will guide the planning process. If you want to write a mystery story, for example, the plot may revolve around a murder, and that will guide much of the planning. Remember, in a short story you don't have the space for multiple major events unless they tie together in theme and lead to a climax.

This is also the time to look for opportunities for foreshadowing. You can use foreshadowing in a short story, as long as you have a delicate touch. You must be subtle, because the reader is generally reading the story at one sitting and is likely to remember everything that came before. There is less camouflage available for your clues.

One excellent source for ideas is your own inner fears or dreams. Think about emotional triggers—a time you hit someone (or were hit), a grand plan that went up in smoke, the first time you said, "I love you," a moment of defeat, a time you feared for your life, something you did that made you ashamed. What makes you cry in movies? Is it father/daughter or mother/son scenes? Lost love? What makes you angry? Is it the person who makes you feel stupid? Being frustrated from achieving a goal? Seeing someone you care about mistreated?

Phrases can trigger story ideas. Think of emotion-packed lines such as, "Please don't hurt me," "I've had it with your lies," or "How could you do that to my sister?" These can be the basis for a character, a key scene, or even the premise of the story.

You can use real life as a starting point, but don't let the truth get in the way of a good story. All writers draw from their own experiences, but with fiction you don't have to keep strictly to the facts. Be creative. Examine events from your life and remember a feeling you had (guilt, humiliation, joy, anger), and then consider what might have happened if you'd made a different choice. You can also use something that happened to someone you know (or you read about in the newspaper). Just be sure to disguise the details adequately.

Obituaries can be excellent sources for character names and backstories. Items in antique stores can provide ideas for occupations, props for characters, or details for settings. Online sites such as Pinterest can provide ideas, as long as you don't wake up three hours later and realize you've created some impressive boards for vintage hats, pie recipes, and craft projects but haven't gotten any further along on your story.

Although it's easier to write about things you already know (places you've lived or visited, jobs you've held, experiences you've had), some people prefer to choose something they know nothing about and do enough research to write about it convincingly.

The traditional advice of "write what you know" has value because when the writer has firsthand knowledge, the writing tends to be more detailed and vivid than that derived completely from research or the imagination. Look for ways your special expertise will add authenticity. Are you an avid collector of something? Have you spent time living in a particular area? Had an unusual experience? Think about how you can weave bits of this knowledge into your writing. Don't bury readers with a deluge of explanation, but a few authentic details can add spark to a story. This can be in the form of inside knowledge, specialized terms, or character details.

Write what you know, but don't feel you have to stay in your comfort zone. If all writers stuck to firsthand experience, we'd never have science fiction, fantasy, or stories in which characters get good cable service.

Keep an idea file of news clippings, overheard conversations, photographs of locations you may want to use, maps, and other resources that might come in handy for your writing projects. Always be thinking, "what if?"

Getting Started Checklist

❒ Have you given some thought to the potential market for your story?

❒ Do you have a place to write that suits your needs?

❒ Have you decided on the type of story you want to write?

❒ Are you reading high-quality short stories for education and inspiration?

❒ Have you mined your own experiences for ideas?

❒ Do you have an idea file for collecting photos, articles, and notes for future stories?

❒ Have you developed at least a basic synopsis for the story?

The Importance of Story

I'll call anything a story in which specific characters and events influence each other to form a meaningful narrative.

–Flannery O'Connor, "The Nature and Aim of Fiction"

Seinfeld may have been "a show about nothing," but look at any episode and you will find a story. An inconsequential story, perhaps, but a story. A narrative in which nothing happens would have little appeal to viewers. In real life, something is always happening.

One of the most common flaws I see in contest entries is the most basic—no story. It's right there in the title: short *story*. Just because it's short doesn't mean it can get by without something happening. A chronological what-I-did-on-my-summer-vacation narrative is not a story. A list of childhood memories, no matter how poetically they are described, is not a story. A description of an event is not a story. A wandering travelogue is not a story—unless *something happens*.

A story has characters, conflict, action, and resolution. It has plot. It nearly always has dialogue. If your story has a "first I did this, then I did that" format, it is likely not a story. If your story is simply a description of an event, it is likely not a story. There must be a conflict, an emotional effect, a transformation.

Story requires at least one character. The character must want something and need to take action in order to get it. Usually, something or somebody stands in the way, providing the conflict or problem. A character watching events unfold is not a story. The conflict or problem is what forces the character to take action and results in some sort of change that leads to the story's resolution. As Steven James says, "Simply put, you do not have a story until something goes wrong."

Some writers get confused about the difference between an idea and a plot. An idea might be writing about your first trip to the beach. A plot might be (based on that memory) a character making a first trip to the beach for a desperately needed vacation who runs into an ex-boss who is now working at a food stand to make ends meet. What that character does, how he or she interacts with the ex-boss, and how the vacation turns out becomes a story.

Anne Leigh Parrish, fiction editor for *Eclectica* magazine, says, "A story is not a nice description of how things are. It's not a sensibility, or a mood. While those elements surely contribute to a story, a story itself is a narrative where there must be a change in the reader's understanding of the events, or in the protagonist's understanding. You leave a story seeing something you didn't see at the outset, something that makes sense of what's come before."

A story starts with a problem. The problem may be quite small, but must be significant enough to provide the foundation for a story. One way to develop an idea is to take a common situation and then ask "what if?" Nancy Powichroski Sherman was writing *Sandy Shorts*, a collection of short beach reads, when she took the common situation of people coming to the beach to stay in a rental house. She asked this question: "What if two sets of people were mistakenly given the same rental house for the week?" It became a romantic romp featuring a group of gal pals that find their rental home already inhabited by a group of men who refuse to vacate. Simple problem, but lots of room for fun.

Look for problems and motivations that are universal or at least that many readers can identify with in a general sense. For example, readers may not have had a drunk driver kill their child, but they can identify with the rage and desire for revenge that can result from such a situation. Readers may not have seriously considered murdering their spouses or employers, but most people can identify with the anger, jealousy, or frustration that leads to murderous thoughts.

The story must be credible. If your characters take extraordinary actions, make sure there is adequate motivation and explanation. For example, if your female character is going to successfully fight off several attackers, plant some information earlier in the story about her background (four brothers), training (karate), or motivation (she had been attacked before and vowed never to be a victim again). If you need a character out of the way, find a convincing errand to send him on. If you need a character in a scene, make sure there is a reason why she would be there. Coincidences do happen, but not just to make the writer's job easier. Readers tend to be skeptical of convenient coincidences, so it's better to lay some groundwork that makes a chance meeting seem more plausible, or a random discovery more likely.

As you develop your story, look for an opportunity to create a twist. How can you surprise the reader, while still playing fair with the information given? Know from the beginning what the twist will be and drop tiny hints along the way. A convincing, yet surprising twist is a wonderful way to end a story.

The Beginning

> **As it is in chess, so it is in fiction, you must command the beginning game before you can handle the middle, or even consider the end.**
>
> –Jack Webb, "In the Beginning"

Have you ever opened a book, taken a look at the first line or two, and then either kept reading or put it down? If you're like most people, you have. Well, like it or not, many readers (including—perhaps even especially—editors and agents) will do exactly that with your short story. After all that work on characters, plot, setting, and structure, if your first few lines don't sing, the reader will never get to the chorus.

When you get ready to write, you may get yourself a cup of coffee, turn on your work light, boot up your computer, adjust your chair, stretch out your arms, and perhaps wiggle your fingers in anticipation. You open a new document, perhaps set a font and type size, and begin typing. If you were being profiled on television, do you think they would show all that? No. It's boring and unnecessary. That's why you shouldn't make your readers sit through your story's preparation.

The first few sentences of your story determine whether readers continue to read. Is this story going to be compelling? Do I care about the character(s)? Is it set in a time and place that interests me? Is it worth my time to read? Like the tantalizing displays you see as you walk into a store, the beginning is where you place your most enticing wares in hopes that the customer will pick it up and think, "Ah, this is for me." If you feel you need to start at the beginning, go ahead. But once you start to edit, remove (or move) that initial arm stretching and finger wiggling.

Never start with backstory. Background information can be divulged in bits and pieces along the way. Start with a conflict or threat, something unusual or unexpected, an intriguing conversation, or just about anything that will make the reader want to find out more. Put characters (especially the main character) in motion quickly. Grab and emotionally hook the reader immediately. Be inside the character's head, reacting and being reacted to as quickly as possible. Establish the time and place within the first few paragraphs, but don't open with description or scene-setting narration.

> Compare this: "It was a warm day in September. Claire pushed her long blond hair off her face as she closed the door to her tidy Nantucket bungalow. She had lived on the island for six years. As she got to her car, she noticed that the tires were flat."

> With this: "Slashed tires. Again. Claire gazed up the quiet Nantucket street. In six years, she had never had a problem. Until now."

One of the best ways to hook the reader is to open in the middle of the action, which provides excitement and curiosity. How did this happen? What's going on here? You might open in the middle of a conversation, which provides insights into the characters, reveals something about the setting, and hints at the conflict. You might open with the setting in a way that creates fear, curiosity, or other emotions. This is a particularly effective way to open a story in which the setting plays a major role, but works only with a distinctive setting that creates atmosphere for the story. You might open with a question, and then immediately move to another scene, leaving the question unanswered for the moment. Just make sure that you ground the reader quickly and provide clues to the location so the characters don't seem to be floating around in space.

Ideally, your story should hook the reader from one section to the next, one paragraph to the next, and even one sentence to the next. Each break, particularly those at the end of a section or paragraph, provides an opportunity for the reader to put the book down. Do you have to put a cliffhanger at the end of every section and every paragraph? No. But think about how you are linking from one paragraph to the next and carrying the reader along. Good transitions move the story forward and keep the reader hooked.

In a short story, you need to get off to a fast start and accomplish a lot quickly. You must grab the reader's attention, provide a sense of time and place, draw the reader into the world you have created, establish the tone of the story, and set the stage for the problem or conflict. You will want to include some tantalizing details, an unanswered question, and a character to root for.

One approach to creating a captivating beginning is to simply write the story, and then go back and think about where the best place would be to *open* the story. It may not be where you started; it may be a few paragraphs or even pages into your initial telling. If you decide you do want to open where you started the story, look within the story for something you can pull out and use at the beginning. It might be foreshadowing, a character insight, unspoken thoughts (the character anticipating what is coming), or a minor prop that becomes important later in the story.

Some authors like to open a story at the first action sequence. In a murder mystery, this might be when the body is discovered or as the murder takes place. Another option is to open with the scene you like the best. You probably like it because it's interesting and well-written, and your readers will like it for those reasons as well. Another approach is to start at the end and then backtrack.

Ring Lardner noticed that some writers always start their stories in a particular way. Jack Dempsey, according to Lardner, starts his stories with "I," while Charley Peterson starts with "a couple of simple declarative sentences about his leading character." As for himself, Larder says, "Personally, it has been my observation that the reading public prefers short dialogue to any other kind of writing and I always aim to open my tale with two or three lines of conversation between characters."

Deciding where to start a story is one of the most important decisions you will make. Remember that the beginning is not what happens before the story starts, it's what happens *when* the story starts. Whatever you choose, start with a scene that tells the reader something about the main character, gives the reader a sense for the story (Will it be funny or sad? Is it a fantasy or a detective story?), and hooks readers so you can then go back and fill in some backstory without losing them. The opening should clue the reader in to the setting, voice, style, and mood of the story and set the table for the feast that is to come.

The Central Conflict

> Everybody thinks he knows what a story is. But if you ask a beginning student to write a story, you're liable to get almost anything—a reminiscence, an episode, an opinion, an anecdote, anything under the sun but a story. A story is a complete dramatic action—and in good stories, the characters are shown through the action and the action is controlled through the characters, and the result of this is meaning that derives from the whole presented experience.
>
> –Flannery O'Connor, "Writing Short Stories"

Beginning writers often find themselves writing happy stories. After all, who doesn't like it when good things happen? Their character goes through the story, interacts with other characters, and good things happen. The end. Sounds boring, doesn't it? That's because it *is* boring. Despite what you might think, people like reading about problems: challenges, conflicts, danger, and seemingly insurmountable difficulties. Your character facing one or more problems, failing at first, and then finding a solution is what makes a story.

According to Jack Bickham, "Most short fiction falls into one of three categories: stories of *conflict*, stories of *decision*, or stories of *discovery*...The story of conflict is the record of a goal-motivated fight. The story of decision is the record of an agonized search for new direction. The story of discovery is the record of a pilgrim's blind wandering until a life-changing discovery, perhaps very tiny indeed, is made." The type of story you choose will affect the kinds of characters (and their traits) that populate the story.

A winning story relies on a central conflict—something for the character to solve, overcome, or be consumed by. The problem also provides a reason for the reader to care, gets the reader's interest, and creates curiosity. Conflict propels the character to action. In a short story, the problem cannot be so big that it can't be resolved within the space of a short story. Have one central problem and let other story lines wrap around it. There is not enough room for multiple problems unless they are connected.

Create the problem, then raise the stakes. Introduce an obstacle that prevents the character from achieving the goal. The conflict can be internal or external, can be between characters or within a character, or can involve an external force. Obstacles can be another character (antagonist), time, space, a personality flaw, or another factor that stands between the character and the goal. The obstacles could be unintended consequences of decisions the character makes, which force another choice, which may lead to additional problems. Each failure should have consequences to build tension, but should be a small step toward the solution.

Chris Winkle advises writers to "give each failed attempt a small step toward the solution. It might be clue, a tool, or a piece of advice that will help your character. That doesn't mean they'll recognize it right away. In fact, it's better if they don't."

Stories of conflict generally involve two characters who oppose each other or who are trying to reach conflicting goals. The classic example is the hero/villain tale that leads up to a dramatic battle of some kind, after which one wins and one loses. Although the conflict can be more subtle than that, there is usually a clear winner and a clear loser.

In stories of decision, the conflict can be internal. The character may be forced into a choice, face a life-changing turning point, or have to deal with a serious interpersonal problem that needs resolution. Stories of discovery may be even more internal. The character may find some sort of inner strength or discover something life-changing. It may be unclear what the character is seeking or that the character is seeking anything at all, until the discovery is made. And the discovery itself can be quite small, but it must matter to the character. The more important the discovery is to the character, the more important it is to the reader. Increase the interest level by creating ambiguity. Leave some things unclear: Is it a ghost or a delusion? Did she jump off the bridge or just think about it?

Want to bump up the tension? Put a clock on it. Create a deadline that must be met, whether it's a race to defuse a bomb or *An Affair to Remember*, an all-or-nothing romantic rendezvous. Look for what Sarah Hall calls "rug-pull moments." The tension in the story should lead to a pivotal scene—the climax of the story. The climax should not be rushed, as much of the reader's enjoyment of the story depends on how well the key incident of the story is told.

Details, Details, Details

> **Short stories can be rather stark and bare unless you put in the right details. Details make stories human, and the more human a story can be, the better.**
>
> –V. S. Pritchett, quoted in "Ordinary Life Always Went Too Far"

As you write your story, include as many details as possible. And not just any details—specific, individual, telling details about the setting, characters, emotions, and situation. Editor and publisher Sol Stein uses the term *particularity*. If the character is wearing a coat, what kind of coat is it? Is it a fur-lined parka? A velvet-trimmed opera jacket? A torn hoodie? Details bring a story to life and help readers set their mind stage for the events. The best details go another step and reveal character, illuminate emotion, and help drive the story.

When selecting details, include all the senses. Beginning writers tend to focus on the visual, but other senses can be much more evocative. The sense of smell, for example, is intimately connected to memory. Look for offbeat, less common but more informative sensory details. The waxy scent of an old coloring book (childhood memories) rather than the musty smell of the cabinet (just conveys age). Sense of touch can tell us about characters (the feel of a handshake), setting (damp towels), and even plot (a scarf wrapping around the neck).

Taste details can also tap memories (strawberries that bring back grandma's garden) and add depth to the story. And don't forget to bring in sound, a constant presence in our lives. Just be sure to really *use* your senses. Don't fall back on clichés like "clanging bell," "sweet as a rose," "razor-sharp," and so forth.

Look for slang and specialized, regional, or even foreign terms your readers may not be familiar with to add atmosphere and realism to your story. If you use the words in a context where your readers will be able to figure out their meaning, it will make the readers feel clever and teach them something along the way. For example, if a character is cooking an ethnic dish, include some specific terms for utensils, ingredients, and methods to add authenticity. Even if readers don't know exactly what a term means, they will still get the gist, and it will add "flavor." In fantasy stories (or those with quirky characters), you can even use made-up terms (*truthiness*, anyone?).

Don't confuse obscure vocabulary or inflated verbiage for detail. Stephen King says that looking for long words to replace short ones in your writing is "like dressing up a household pet in evening clothes. The pet is embarrassed and the person who committed this act of premeditated cuteness should be even more embarrassed." Details can be simple and still carry significant weight. They should be precise and, ideally, original. One way to do this is to use words in an unusual context. Sol Stein points to Graham Greene's use of the term *bald* to refer to knees ("bald pink knees") in *The Heart of the Matter* as an example of particularization. "Bald pink head" wouldn't have been nearly as effective, as it's an ordinary description.

When doing your research, look for terms that enrich the story. Just make sure that any details you mention when writing from a character's viewpoint are details that character would be likely to have noticed and recognized. A person on a diet would likely notice how much another person ate at lunch, but an older man would be unlikely to notice that a woman's dress is out of style (unless he's in the clothing business).

The words a character chooses are also telling. A farmer observing the weather would use different words than a sailor, a storm chaser, an event planner, or a meteorologist. A handyman would use different words to describe building features than an architect or an interior designer. If your character is a botanist or even an experienced gardener, she's not going to refer to a plant as a "bush." She'd be more likely to say "shrub," "beautyberry," or even "*Callicarpa dichotoma*."

Technical terms used by technical people provide depth and

legitimacy. A story about sailing could include some boating terms. A character who is a hobbyist might name a specific type of tool or method. Also look for regional terms ("catawampus," "pinkletink," or even "whoopensocker") and generational slang, occupational terms, geographic/topographic details, or architectural terms.

When describing characters, make the description do double-duty. Description should allow the reader to form a visual, but should also tell us about the character's personality and background. The reader doesn't need to know everything the character is wearing, but a few well-chosen details can be revealing. Descriptions given through the eyes of another character filter the perception with attitudes, prejudices, and background. A parent would describe a teenage daughter's tattoo in a different way than the daughter's best friend. Don't limit your details to adjectives. You can show detail in many ways. Instead of writing that someone had a loud sneeze, you could describe a startled bystander or have a character question whether her sneezes are the reason the pictures on the wall are crooked.

Add mystery by withholding some details. If you're writing a story involving a historical event, consider just starting the story without telling the reader the exact date. Like the movie that shows people having fun on a ship before pulling back and revealing the life preserver with *Titanic* written on it, your story will pack more punch if readers are taken off guard. Consider withholding a key piece of information, a relationship between two characters, a past event, or other information that will have the reader wondering for a while. A little misdirection (keep it fair) can confound your character and delay satisfaction.

Remember that your characters are living in the moment. They don't know what's coming and shouldn't act as though they are anticipating it. Use the element of surprise whenever you can. It will be all the more powerful for your readers.

Details are particularly important when writing humor. It's difficult to make a green vegetable funny, but change it to a pickle or a zucchini and you're in business. Details also allow you to exaggerate—a key element of humor.

Use dialogue and action to bring your story to life. But when you must explain, include telling details and have those details do extra duty— indicate character attributes, reveal conflict, uncover secrets, and add mystery. Details—especially *telling* details—add richness to the story, dimension to the characters, and liveliness to the setting.

Illustration vs. Explanation

> Don't tell me the moon is shining. Show me moonlight reflected on broken glass.
>
> –Anton Chekov

There seems to be a natural inclination, especially among beginning writers, to "tell a story." This sort of writing opens with an implied, "Once upon a time," and then sets the scene, describes the main characters, and explains what is going on. Imagine the equivalent in the art world: "This painting is a seaside scene. There is a middle-aged man wearing tan shorts and a blue shirt, and a woman with a large hat. The man and woman are getting into a boat." Would that do it for you, or would you rather actually see the painting?

Look for ways to illustrate rather than narrate (that's another way of saying "show, don't tell"). Why does everyone say that? What's so wrong with telling? If you were going to Italy on vacation, would you rather hear about it from a tour guide or smell the steaming marinara sauce and taste the Chianti for yourself? People like to *experience* things, not just be told about them. Rather than write, "It was a dark and stormy night," let the reader hear thunder, smell ozone, and struggle to get the umbrella up.

That doesn't mean that you must avoid all explanation. There are times (and this is particularly true with short stories) when you won't want to show everything. You want to save the showing for the most dramatic, story-advancing scenes. We don't need to see the character running to the store, changing clothes, or dropping the kids off at school, unless it plays an important part in the story.

Check your writing for instances where you have described emotions, character attributes (especially personality), or setting that could be illustrated instead. If you find yourself writing something involving emotions ("James was angry"), look for ways to show this through action ("James threw the car keys at Sarah") or dialogue ("'Get out,' James shouted."). Character traits such moodiness, thrift, kindness, impatience, disorganization, and the like can be conveyed through action ("He scooped up the fast food containers, mail, and other debris from the passenger seat and tossed it into the back to make room."). Setting, especially weather, can be described through actions (putting on gloves, wiping sweat) or dialogue ("You're so lucky to have a view of the sea.").

Here is an excerpt from Barbara Holland's memoir, *When All the World Was Young*, that is loaded with explanation—of characters, relationships, even setting—yet it telegraphs the information in a way that draws readers in rather than pushing them away: "She [Mother] came into the house and sat down with her raincoat still belted, perched on the edge of the couch like a social worker, and she and Grandmother discussed whatever it was. Mother was using her formal voice, the guarded one she used on bus drivers and automobile mechanics...This *was* her mother, wasn't it?"

Resist the urge to explain (editors sometimes mark manuscripts with "R.U.E." to remind writers about this) and make sure you're not telling readers things you've already shown through dialogue and action. Dialogue and action, when carefully constructed, can carry a lot of narrative weight as long as you don't try to pile on too much too fast. Look for ways to get your readers into the story and to let them experience it for themselves. Readers are smarter than you think. Have the confidence to trust them.

The Ending

> To me, the ending felt so correct and so appropriate that it seemed to bend over backward to kiss the beginning.
>
> –Elizabeth Gilbert, "The Lousy Rider"

A problem I often see in short stories submitted to the Rehoboth Beach Reads Short Story Contest is a poor ending. Sometimes I get the feeling that the writer, having struggled to get the story, structure, setting, characters, dialogue, and other factors right, just wanted to be done with it already. But the ending is where the reader either slowly pushes back from the dinner table, savoring the story with a smile, or bolts from the table to turn on the television.

A good ending satisfies the reader, is in keeping with the genre and mood, makes sense and is plausible for the characters and the story, and contains a bit of a surprise or a revelation (not be too predictable).

The ending should carry a weight commensurate with the depth of its subject matter and theme. A light story about a talking dog might have a short, funny twist at the end; whereas, a story that explored the concept of prejudice warrants a thoughtful, well-paced conclusion. Edith Wharton said, "As every subject contains its own dimensions, so is its conclusion *ab ovo*; and the failure to end a tale in accordance with its own deepest sense must deprive it of meaning."

Even in a short story, take a little time with the ending. Time doesn't necessarily mean length, but have enough of an ending that it doesn't feel as though you're dropping the story like a hot casserole lid.

For starters, know where you are headed from the beginning. You wouldn't start a trip by just blindly driving around; you would have at least a general destination in mind. If you start writing a story without knowing where you are headed, you will end up with a story that wanders around, takes wrong turns, wastes precious time, and leaves the reader confused.

The ending should resolve the central conflict. It doesn't have to answer every question, but it should satisfy the reader. Ideally, the resolution arises naturally from the conflict in the story.

The ending can provide insight into the theme. It can surprise or shock the reader. It can show how the character has evolved. It can circle back to something at the beginning of the story.

If the character has been transformed, don't stop at the transformation. Show us the results. How does the character see the world and himself differently at the end of the story?

Allow readers to take a breath and come to terms with the ending. Let them down gently. A satisfying ending makes readers want to linger a little. And take particular care with the final sentence. The last line of a story is as important as the first. A memorable last line sticks in the reader's mind.

At the other end of the spectrum is the writer who just can't say goodbye. A telltale sign for me is the contest submission that comes in at 3,499 words when the limit is 3,500. These endings blather on, giving the reader too much information, taking the reader beyond the natural ending point, or just using too many words in too many ways to say "the end."

If your ending seems too drawn out, try leaving some details to the reader's imagination. Readers have minds of their own. If you point a despondent character toward the ocean at night, readers get it. You don't have to fill the character's pockets with rocks and get her feet wet.

See if there are places where you can remove some description or explanation. The ending isn't the place to be telling the reader about the setting, the weather, or the character's traits.

If you are having trouble coming up with an ending at all, make sure you really have a story. A story has something for the character to solve, overcome, or be consumed by. It's the character's fight to resolve this central conflict that makes the story that gets resolved in the end.

Endings don't have to be neat. Leave something to the reader's imagination. The ending can leave the reader with a question or a series of questions rather than just answers. Like poetry, a short story can be thought-provoking and engaging, without necessarily telling the entire story, which is often the expectation of a novel. Ask a question—a rhetorical question that restates the theme or summarizes the story.

Stay away from endings that are too pretty and buttoned down (they lived happily ever after) or clichéd (and then he woke up!), or that leave loose ends without explanation (what happened to the loaded gun she left on the table?).

Also stay away from "the moral of the story" endings. You don't have to tell the reader what it all means. Take the story into a higher plane—interpret the events of the story into a broader context—but be careful not to lecture or explain too much. A little goes a long way. You're writing a story, not giving a sermon.

Ideally, the beginning of the story should forecast the end. Think of it like bookends—take a phrase, image, location, or action from the beginning of the story and echo it at the end. This technique works particularly well if there is clearly a change that involves the character coming around (new information, irony, character growth, or change in circumstances). The repetition can be the same or have important changes (a different result, an object at the beginning is now broken, a character is now dead).

In Kathleen L. Martens's story "Molting" from the anthology *Beach Days*, a ticking clock in the first paragraph symbolizes the predicable, planned life her character longs to escape. The clock reappears at the end of the story, where it offers reassurance and comfort. By framing the beginning and the ending, the story seems to come full circle, and the ending is satisfying.

T. S. Eliot said, "In my beginning is my end." If the resolution arises naturally from the conflict, it can help reinforce how much has changed. Discussing Edith Wharton's story "Roman Fever," Barbara A. White says, "Wharton cleverly plants the clues so that at the end of the story, just as at the end of a good mystery, the reader exclaims, 'Of course! I should have known all along.'"

Winning stories have endings that go beyond the ordinary. Take the time to give your story the ending it deserves.

Story Checklist

- ❒ Do you have a story (characters, conflict, action, and resolution)?
- ❒ Have you begun the story in the right place?
- ❒ Have you hooked the reader from the start?
- ❒ Did you ground your reader quickly, without getting bogged down with backstory?
- ❒ Do you have a central conflict?
- ❒ Have you chosen specific, telling details?
- ❒ Have you looked for ways to illustrate rather than explain?
- ❒ Have you ended the story in the right place?
- ❒ Is the ending logical and satisfying?
- ❒ Have you left something to the reader's imagination?

Premise and Theme

A premise...is a statement of what happens to the characters as a result of the actions of a story.

–James N. Frey, *How to Write a Damn Good Novel, II*

The premise of a story is the idea behind it—the starting point. It could be a "what if?" scenario (what if a man who plans to jump off a building gets stuck in the elevator), a reversal (man bites dog), or a seemingly hopeless setup (star-crossed love). The premise may incorporate setting, plot, and characters, but boils down to what the story is about and, ideally, is an original idea or an original take on an old idea.

Sometimes the premise incorporates an argument or point of view—something the writer sets out to prove, such as "drugs are being overprescribed." The premise might be this: "A man hastily marries and then learns that impulsivity is a side effect of a medication he is taking."

In *Writing the Breakout Novel*, Donald Maass lists the key components of a "breakout" premise:

- Plausibility
- Inherent conflict
- Originality
- Gut emotional appeal

As you develop your premise, remind yourself that you are writing a short story. You must balance the need for an original, engaging plot with the reality that you just don't have the space for complex story lines with many characters. Remember Amy Bloom's remark that short story writers are the cat burglars of the writing business—get in, get out, and "accomplish something shocking—and lasting—without throwing around the furniture."

Creating a story premise isn't easy, as it involves distilling an entire story into just a sentence or two. Jeff Lyons says "the process of premise development can be the literary equivalent of skiing the black diamond trail." Lyons proposes this template to get at the core structure of the premise: "[When] some event sparks a character to action, that [character acts] with deliberate purpose [until] that action is opposed by an external force, [leading to] some conclusion." This sort of analysis also helps confirm that you have a workable story.

Once you have formulated a story premise, you can test it on readers to determine if your story will be engaging. The premise line can also help keep you focused as you write, so you don't waste time by getting off track (story creep).

The theme of a story is its underlying message. A story shouldn't be a lecture or a sermon, but people like to find meaning, and they like to feel that their time has been well spent. The meaning of a story is found in its theme. The theme doesn't have to be original—in fact, by nature, themes tend to be known, universal concepts.

What do you want to say to your readers? Is there a message you want to convey (the punishment should fit the crime)? Is there a social concern you feel strongly about (children are growing up too fast)? Do you have a personal dilemma or health issue you care about (elder care)? Have you faced a family crisis or witnessed someone else's (divorce, losing a job)?

In a short story, you cannot have a highly complicated plot, but that doesn't mean that the story must be light and insignificant. "Brokeback Mountain" was a short story. "Goodbye, Columbus" and "The Snows of Kilimanjaro" were short stories. The theme or message can be big, but the story must be a small, specific example.

The theme can figure prominently in the story, or it can be lurking in the background and require some thought on the reader's part to discover. The theme may be the lesson learned such as "there's no place like home," the moral of the story such as "crime doesn't pay," or a classic struggle such as man vs. nature. Sometimes a story also demonstrates a universal truth such as "money can't buy happiness" or "mother knows best." This sort of message is perfectly fine and can add substance to the story, but use a light hand and resist the temptation to include the phrase in the story. Nothing is worse than getting to the end of the story and reading, "And that's when she realized that *love is blind*." That's hitting the reader over the head with the theme.

You don't necessarily need to sit down and say, "I'm going to write a story about love being blind," but as you write, try to tap into something significant. Even in a light story, you can touch on themes of importance. Just don't be too obvious; let the reader discover the message, and let elements in the story take on greater meaning.

Flannery O'Connor wrote a story called "Good Country People" in which a bible salesman steals a woman's wooden leg. The story would have been entertaining on its own, but O'Connor made the wooden leg accumulate meaning as the story progressed (the woman is spiritually crippled, and readers perceive there is a wooden part of her soul) so that by the time the salesman takes the leg, it has considerably more significance. The message can arise in the reader's mind as information is revealed. As Ben Nyberg says, "No matter how determined an author may be to sell his ideas, he *never sells direct*."

Theme is often revealed when the characters conflict with each other or when the protagonist faces the central problem or challenge. Cause and effect is what keeps readers involved in the story and invested in its outcome. Each time a character makes a decision, selects a path, or takes action, it changes the trajectory of the story, building toward the conclusion that results from the character's choices. The theme is usually closely related to the outcome of the conflict and can serve as the unstated moral of the story.

Keep your focus small. Your concept can be global, but show it on a local level. If you want to talk about abortion, for example, don't lecture about the issue in general; write a story about someone facing an unplanned pregnancy. And make the characters real, with conflicting ideas, thoughts, and emotions. If your characters become mouthpieces for two opposing points of view, you are writing a script for a debate team, not portraying a realistic situation. If you have a character simply voice your own opinion, you are delivering a lecture and will lose your audience. As an aside, this is seen way too often in children's stories where the characters (even if they are bunnies or kittens) deliver adult lectures about the importance of clean bedrooms and good table manners.

Leslie W. Quirk wrote in *How to Write a Short Story*: "In a short story, absolutely every paragraph, and even every sentence, should be an unfolding and a development of the plot. You must not preach nor teach in your story; not even hint at such things."

You may also find opportunities for symbolism in your story. Symbolism can help tie elements together and create a more powerful effect. It is a way of connecting seemingly unrelated pieces and can also cause the reader to make connections to broader concepts. For example, Stephen King has talked about his use of blood as a symbol in *Carrie*. From Carrie's paranormal ability apparently being brought on by her first menstrual period to the prank involving pig's blood, blood plays more than just its usual role in horror fiction. It's a symbol for sacrifice, for sexual maturity, and for sin and salvation.

Premise and theme create the basis of the story. They encompass what the story "is about" both on the surface and at its core.

PREMISE AND THEME CHECKLIST

- ❒ Have you developed a one- or two-sentence premise?
- ❒ Is your premise plausible?
- ❒ Does the premise interest readers?
- ❒ Have you created a plot that isn't predictable, shallow, or overly complex?
- ❒ Is there an underlying message or universal truth to give readers something to think about?
- ❒ Have you avoided being moralistic and preachy?
- ❒ Have you woven the theme into the story by giving elements within the story greater meaning?
- ❒ Have you looked for opportunities for symbolism?

Structure

Time Frame, Sequence, and Transitions

> The standard shape of a story isn't a straight line. It isn't a straight flat line, it isn't a straight inclined line. Stories have swoops and jiggles and jaggles—it is a craggy and dangerous mountain, not a safe and code-standard wheelchair ramp.
>
> –Chuck Wendig, "In Which I Critique Your Story (That I Haven't Read)"

In a short story, you don't have the space to span centuries; you must focus. Most stories take place over a few hours or days. You can cover a larger span of time, but if you do, focus on one or a limited number of points in time and use flashbacks and flash forwards to add interest and fill in important dramatic scenes. You may also include an epilogue to show future consequences.

Most stories have this sort of progression: we meet the main characters and get a feel for the setting, time period, and voice of the story; action! (some sort of incident or problem emerges—the sooner the better); conflict arises and the character tries to resolve problem or overcome challenge; there is a climax (a break point, a key decision, a dramatic development that forces major change); the characters' actions lead toward the resolution; and then all of this results in a satisfying resolution.

This basic structure dates back to Greek theater and Aristotle, who said that every story has a beginning, a middle, and an end (Greek plays are often in three acts for that reason). The three-act structure is still commonly used but is generally described as rising action, climax, and falling action.

A more modern (mid-1800s) interpretation is Freytag's pyramid (the dramatic arc), which consists of exposition (introduction to characters and setting), rising action (a series of events and complications that provide drama), climax (a turning point where characters either win or lose), falling action (a series of events that lead to the story's conclusion), and the resolution (the end of the story).

Most short stories follow a linear, chronological sequence. It's a logical progression for the story that is easy for readers to follow. For beginning writers, this structure is an ideal place to start:

1. Hook the reader. Set the scene and introduce the main characters. Give the reader a sense of the style, mood, and type of story. Establish the point of view and provide a little background to set up the conflict or complication to come. What does the main character want?

2. Present a complication that stands in the way of the character's goal, an antagonist character that provides conflict, or an event that provides a threat. Ideally, there is a series of escalating complications, which the main character attempts to solve, only to be faced with more roadblocks. (The director Billy Wilder reportedly said that in act one you put your character up a tree and in act two you set the tree on fire.) This middle section generally forces the character to reach a decision that leads toward the solution.

3. Provide a plausible solution, while leaving something for the reader to think about.

Sometimes, even in a linear story, you need to move the story through time or space. The characters are having lunch, but you want to get them to a party that night in another town without having to recount the entire afternoon, the drive over, and the arrival at the party. You need a smooth transition from one scene to the next. The easiest way to indicate a break of time or space is to simply insert space in the manuscript (publishers often use a line of asterisks or a dingbat to indicate a transition).

Another way to signal a change is to use a transitional phrase such as "later that day" or "by summer." You can get more creative by telegraphing the jump without specifically referring to it. Phrases such as "she closed the now-empty cigarette pack" or "New York was surprisingly cold that April" can signal transitions. These phrases may also be accompanied by a graphic clue in the manuscript, but sometimes they can be used without, especially if the jump is a short one.

Be careful not to make transitions too abruptly or your readers may need a neck brace. Indications in dialogue, unspoken thoughts, or narration can warn readers that a jump in time or space is coming. You may also want to give readers a sense of where the story is going and even set the mood for the upcoming scene ("Janet watched droplets of rain hit the windshield. She hoped Luke would be happy to see her." Or "Ellis closed the suitcase and smiled. He wouldn't be needing socks in Key West."). An object can be used to connect two scenes. For example, the next scene might show Ellis unpacking his suitcase in Key West. Weather conditions can also serve as transitions: "As Janet pulled off the Interstate, the rain became steady and the sky darkened."

Transitions can be opportunities to change viewpoint, but be sure to alert the reader immediately. This is best done by starting with the new viewpoint character's name. If the previous scene was told from Janet's point of view, the next scene might open with this transition: "Luke hadn't seen Janet in years. What could she want now?" Transitions do not have to be long (in fact, they shouldn't be), but they are necessary to smoothly move your characters and your story forward, without leaving your reader behind.

A subplot can provide an interesting dimension, as long as it doesn't distract from or obscure the primary story. A subplot can be something going on with a minor character that is revealed as having some significance at the end, or it can be a red herring. It can echo the theme of the main story or be a story within a story—a pearl for the reader to discover. A subplot can add conflict or reveal information about characters in the story. Unfortunately, it is difficult to find room for a subplot in a short story, so unless there is a compelling reason for a subplot, you should focus on the primary story.

Making a Scene

> **Stories are change. They are records of the exceptional...Little Red Riding Hood didn't just walk through the forest—she met the wolf and disobeyed her mother by stopping to talk to him...any kind of writing you're ever likely to do—will turn quickly to ashes if nothing happens. So make something happen and the reader will stay with you. Fail to, and the reader gets bored.**
>
> – Joseph O'Connor, "Joseph O'Connor's Top 10 Tips"

Imagine a film in which the characters just wander around, without really interacting or doing much. It wouldn't be a particularly interesting movie, would it? That's why filmmakers think in terms of "scenes," segments of action in which something happens to advance the story, such as a restaurant scene where we learn that the couple cannot seem to agree on anything, which foreshadows a canceled wedding.

Although you may think scenes are limited to the movies, experienced writers think in terms of scenes, certainly for novels, but even for short stories. A short story may only have a few scenes, but they are still critical for getting the reader wrapped up in the story. Once readers are drawn into a scene, they forget about the writer and become part of the story.

A scene is a story in miniature—told in real time, seen as it occurs, in a specific place and time. It has characters, setting, conflict, and resolution. The key aspect of a scene is that *something happens*. And the thing that happens moves the story forward.

The structure and order of the scenes is essential to the telling of the story. Each scene leads to the next, as the main character moves toward the goal. Within the scene is an immediate problem that must be resolved. For example, the scene might show one character trying to convince another character to do something. There's a longer-term goal, but right now the character *really* needs the other person to go along with the plan. The resolution may actually be a setback, so the character has to try something else (next scene!), or it may be just a partial victory that requires more work. Whatever the resolution, unsettled business pushes the character forward into subsequent scenes.

When thinking in scenes, also think about the follow-up, or sequel, to the scene. That is where the character reacts to the scene and makes a decision that leads to the next scene. Jack Bickham puts it this way: the classic pattern of a scene is "goal…conflict… disaster. The classic pattern of the sequel is emotion…thought… decision." The sequel can be as short as a sentence or two, or it can be several pages, depending on the type of story and the importance of the scene.

Because short stories are, well, short, you may have to make fast transitions of time and space. Don't leave your reader behind. The last sentence of the paragraph should lead to the first sentence of the next paragraph to successfully hand off the transition. For example, the last line of one paragraph might be, "She climbed into the car, set the GPS, and said goodbye to Minneapolis." And the first line of the next paragraph might be, "After two hundred miles and way too much coffee, she needed to find a restroom. Now."

Thinking in terms of scenes will help you visualize your story and will push you to "show, not tell." When you find yourself describing a setting, characters, and action, you probably have a scene that should be "acted out" with dialogue and action. You can summarize a scene through narration, but it's not as interesting as actually seeing it, hearing it, and experiencing it. Scenes are harder to write, but they engage readers in a way that narration really can't. Through scenes you draw your reader into your world, as a fly on the wall, watching the story unfold instead of just hearing about it afterward.

You will still need some breaks between scenes to vary the rhythm and pace of the story and to give readers a chance to digest what has happened. This is where a little narrative can be useful. You also need a way to transition between scenes. Narrative can provide a consistent thread throughout the story that guides the reader. Narrative is also needed to show passage of time, explain things that happen "offstage," and provide background (unless you're showing it as flashback).

Flashbacks

> **Flashbacks are, in a sense, the mirrors which an author holds up to the reader, so that the reader gets a front, side and rear view of the character in the story.**
>
> –Susan Thaler, "How to Use the Flashback in Fiction"

Flashbacks can be used to show, rather than explain, what happened in the past. Flashbacks can be particularly helpful when you want to start the story in the middle of the action, but need to fill in some of the background to provide context and meaning. They can also be used to show incidents from the past that are relevant to the present situation.

It is increasingly common for stories (whether print or film) to skip around in time. For this reason, the breaks between scenes (extra space, sometimes accompanied by a line of stars or a graphic element) can help the reader recognize when the story jumps back (or forward) in time.

Flashbacks hold up the action. They are a way of saying, "Wait a minute, let me explain how this happened." For this reason, they can slow the pace of a story. However, they can also add immediacy to background information important to the story.

Choose flashbacks wisely. A flashback scene should add depth and dimension to a key character and be integral to the action, important to the plot, and dramatic in the telling. The character having breakfast that morning? Probably not worthy of a flashback. The character nearly getting hit by a car that turns out to be driven by the character's ex-husband? Could make for a dramatic flashback. Flashbacks are often the best way to effectively convey information from the distant past. Short stories normally have a fairly short time frame, so if an incident from ten years ago is important, you will not be able to include that scene easily in a linear time line.

When you use a flashback, be sure to give the reader a warning so it is clear when the flashback starts and when it ends. As long as you have established that your characters are in the past, you do not need to change tense; you can treat the scene as if it's happening now. The first sentence should telegraph the flashback and be compelling, but transition the reader as unobtrusively as possible. You can get into the flashback by using a transition phrase ("Her first date with him hadn't gone well…") or insert space to indicate a shift in time and start with a time stamp ("Earlier that year"). Immediately get into the same tense as the story (don't get hung up with "hads": "I had been…"). Use dialogue to get into the action quickly.

It is equally important to bring the reader back into the main story. You can signal the end of a flashback with some blank lines to mark the passage of time, words that indicate time ("The next day"), or by referencing the flashback in current time ("Yesterday, when you said…").

Remember that flashbacks break the narrative so they also break the reading experience. The reader is fully engaged with the character and engrossed in the story, waiting to see what happens next, when there's a tap on the shoulder and a "hey, look over here." For this reason, flashbacks should only be used to provide essential insights that enhance the story, show an entire scene (ideally showing characters in conflict), and be witnessed in present time. Before writing a flashback, look for ways to convey the necessary information within the main story.

Pacing

> **Every flower blooms at a different pace.**
>
> –Suzy Kassem, *Rise Up and Salute the Sun: The Writings of Suzy Kassem*

Short stories move at a faster pace, in general, than novels. There is no room for filler. Scenes and dialogue that don't advance the plot or provide character insights should be removed to keep the story on track. Every scene, every character, and every sentence should serve a purpose.

Pacing provides an up-and-down modulation or rhythm to the story that varies strong, emotional, or exciting scenes with reflective, interpretive, or letdown periods. Even with a short story, the reader needs time to absorb and understand intense scenes. Unrelenting tension is exhausting, and unrelieved relaxation is boring (at least that's what I tell my husband when there are chores to be done).

Things that control pacing include the following:

- Number of scenes and their lengths
- Dialogue
- Unspoken thoughts
- Word and sentence structure (and length)
- Transitions

Pacing affects suspense, humor, emotional impact, and engagement. If your pacing is too slow, you may bore (or lose) your readers. If it's too fast, you run the risk of wearing them out. Avoid unrelenting misery or unending hilarity. Give readers a break. Even a dark story should offer some element of hope or at least a lesson learned.

Different types of stories require different pacing. An introspective story will have more leisurely pacing than a thriller, but there still should be some rhythm and variation in pace. If nothing else, you can change the pace by including flashbacks or flash forwards, adding sections of dialogue, or shortening or lengthening scenes.

Action, narrative, and dialogue should work together to move the story along. Decide what should be shown and what can take place in the background. Don't skim over important scenes, and don't drag scenes out. If you are writing about a cop investigating a murder, we don't need to see him getting up in the morning, putting on his uniform (well, that *might* be interesting…), and driving to the scene unless what happens is important to the story. Keep moving, but give the reader some places to take a breath. Take a breath, not go to sleep.

While each scene should have some tension, make sure the pivotal scenes have the most tension and the scenes on either side of them have significant—if subtle—tension of their own. Everything must advance the story, so be selective. This is particularly difficult to do when you are writing about your own experiences. You have to consider the fact that what was important to you in your own life may not be important to others. Keep only the parts that are relevant to the story you're telling.

Pacing is hard to judge until the story is complete. This is yet another reason for getting your first draft down before tinkering too much with the story. Check pacing by reading the story aloud or having others read it. Increase pace by cutting a scene to condense time, starting the story closer to the end, shortening sentences, removing some adverbs and adjectives, using active voice, adding dialogue, increasing action, and reducing explanation. Reduce pace by adding more narrative and details, including a flashback, lengthening sentences, reducing dialogue, adding a distraction or setback, or including thoughts and reflection.

Consider proportion when you look at pacing. If an element in the story isn't terribly significant, you shouldn't spend three or four pages on it. Unless you are writing a mystery and want to intentionally mislead the reader, spend time on the parts of the story that carry the most significance. You may also mislead readers if you spend too much time on a particular character, a relationship between characters, or a plot point that is not important.

Proportion also becomes a concern when you are explaining. Most people today would say that Herman Melville spent just a bit too much time describing whaling in his book *Moby-Dick; or, The Whale.* You may have done a tremendous amount of research to make sure that your setting is accurate, your historical details correct, and your explanations of specialized materials precise, but your readers won't want to have to slog through every bit of it to get to your story. Be particularly careful when describing something you yourself love. You will have a much higher tolerance for a subject that interests you than your readers will.

Structure Checklist

❒ Have you determined a logical sequence for the story?

❒ Does your story have a nice rhythm, with intense scenes, followed by short periods of letdown or reflection?

❒ Have you looked for opportunities to use scenes to tell the story?

❒ Are transitions clear and smooth?

❒ Are any flashbacks necessary and well chosen?

❒ Have you made it clear where flashbacks start and stop?

❒ Does tension build throughout the story?

❒ Does the pacing of the story match its content?

❒ Does the plot move forward at a speed that maintains reader interest?

❒ Did you devote more space to the most significant characters and scenes?

Setting

A short story must have a single mood and every sentence must build towards it.

–attributed to Edgar Allan Poe

The story's setting should be chosen with just as much care as the characters—not only the geographic location, but also the time of year, hour of day, specific location, and reason the characters are there.

You must first decide where and when your story takes place. You can choose to set your story in present day, in the past, or in the future. The past can be just a few years ago, or it can be a historical period such as Colonial America, Renaissance Europe, or the Cold War era. If your story is set in the future, you may want to set it in a recognizable location (New York), or you can create an imaginary location (Planet Yron). The same story will have a different feel, depending on where you set it. Imagine a contemporary murder mystery set in a rough part of Philadelphia. Now imagine the same story in New Orleans, Las Vegas, Miami, or Washington, DC. Each location provides a different opportunity for evocative details.

Next you must decide the specific location or locations within that when and where. The place where your story unfolds affects the characters and how they react. If the characters are in a house, what kind of house? What room in the house? Imagine a bickering couple. An argument in the garage will be different from one in the bedroom. Is it a hot day or cold? How did the characters get there? Are some characters more comfortable in the setting than others?

The setting is not just a stage or a backdrop. And it's more than just props. What is the quality of light? The sun, fluorescent bulbs, table lamps, candles, and computer screens all generate different colors and quantities of light and can contribute to the story. Is it hot and muggy or cold and dreary? Weather can affect mood as can clothing, transportation, and interactions. Just make sure that the weather is plausible for the specific time and place. What social and cultural clues are present? Does the character keep the heat low out of environmental concern or because the trust fund has run out?

Have the characters interact with elements of the setting; the reader should see the setting through the character's eyes. You can convey geography in how the character gets from one place to another (climbing hills, riding the subway, driving through miles of prairie). Climate will affect how the character dresses and details such as opening windows, turning on the air conditioning, or tossing a bag of road salt in the car.

Use setting to telegraph mood. English novelist Edward Bulwer-Lytton was mocked for his use of the opening line, "It was a dark and stormy night," but with an opening like that, the reader immediately knows that the characters in the story may face some challenges. Contrast the Bulwer-Lytton line with the opening sentence of George Orwell's *1984*: "It was a bright cold day in April, and the clocks were striking thirteen." One can almost see the readers' heads snapping back as they realize this is no ordinary setting.

The other component of setting is the span of time and space. Just as a short time period will add immediacy and tension, a small setting (all of the events taking place in one constrained area) will add focus and intensity to a story. The best example for this is *Lifeboat*, a film by Alfred Hitchcock in which the entire film (which includes a murder) takes place on a small lifeboat. Talk about tension.

If the setting is specialized (a nursing home, police station, medical laboratory, archeological dig), visit one or more actual locations so you get the details right. If you have a character drive from one place to another, find out how long it takes to get there (at that time of day) so you don't have someone listening to an hour-long podcast during a trip that takes ten minutes or have someone zipping down a road that gets jammed up with traffic when the factory shift changes or school lets out. If the character takes public transportation, verify the route, time, and day of the week. Even in fiction, the details must be accurate.

Research any activities you describe, along with their associated traditions and practices. For example, if you have the captain of a fishing charter boat munching on a banana as the boat leaves the dock, readers who are sport fishermen are likely to toss your book overboard (bananas are considered bad luck on fishing boats—something a charter captain would surely know).

The objects in a scene are more than just set decoration; they can convey information. A character's office, kitchen, bathroom, or bedroom can tell us much about him or her. There can be incongruity (as in life)—someone might have a sparkling clean kitchen but a messy office. A character might eat on paper plates but have silver candlesticks. Details make a setting come to life, but be sure to use details that give the reader information. For example, we don't care what kind of pants the character wears unless it tells us something about the character or the setting.

Describe the trees and other natural features, but make sure you have your facts right. Plants that grow well in your yard might not be found near the sea or in the mountains. Plants also have different forms at different times of the year. In early spring, some may be flowering; others may be in bud; and still others may not have emerged from the ground. Bodies of water also change seasonally.

Make sure you know the setting well. Do more research than you think you will need. Places change, so don't rely on your memory. Revisit locations to confirm the existence of any buildings, streets, monuments, restaurants, or other features you reference if you are using a real place. Get one detail wrong and your readers will be whisked right out of the story. What? There's no eighteenth floor in that building!

If you set your story in another time period, research will be particularly important. Towns get larger (or smaller) over time. Manners, dress, speech, activities, and habits are considerably different for people living in 1820, 1940, 1982, or 2015.

Just because you learned something through research doesn't mean you have to put it in the story. Avoid the info dump, which slows down the story, interrupts immersion in the fictional world, and bores the reader. And remember that you don't have to reveal every detail of the setting in the first couple of paragraphs. Even in a short story, you can dole out details along the way and let the reader discover more about the setting as the story progresses.

Setting Checklist

❐ Have you carefully selected a setting that is a perfect fit for the story?

❐ Have you used the setting to help establish mood?

❐ Do you have the characters interacting with the setting?

❐ Have you researched the location to make sure the details are accurate?

❐ Have you conveyed the setting over the course of the story rather than in one info dump?

Characters

Choosing Characters

> A character seems alive for you as a reader when you realize him with your senses, react to him with your emotions, follow him with your mind.
>
> –Pearl Hogrefe, "Bringing Characters to Life"

A short story cannot have a cast of thousands; there simply isn't room. By the time you introduce a few characters and have them really mixing it up, it's nearly time to start wrapping up the story. For this reason, most short stories have no more than three or four characters. Limiting the number of characters helps focus the story on the central conflict or problem. And sharp focus, be it in a photograph or a short story, is what you want.

A place to start is with one main character (usually the one whose viewpoint is used to tell the story) and two supporting characters, at least one of whom is an antagonist (a character standing in the way of the main character's goal). The love triangle is a classic form of this configuration.

The main character should be someone your readers will care about—someone they can identify with, root for, and see the story through. He or she does not have to be perfect (and shouldn't be—that would be unrealistic and will actually make the character harder for readers to identify with), but should be sympathetic and generally likeable. Make sure you really *know* the character so you can accurately depict actions and reactions based on motivation, personality, and background.

Ideally, you have a primary character who is complex (multidimensional), has a burning desire and/or a fundamental fear, and carries some baggage (secrets, embarrassing past, feelings of regret or guilt). Aim for a character that the reader is dying to know more about and can identify with in some way.

One way to get a reader to identify with a character is to generate a problem for the character that is not of his or her own making. We all face external problems that block us from achieving our goals. These can range from big problems (death or infidelity of a spouse, illness, or serious issues with children) to small problems (a missed date, car breakdown, or computer crash). And of course sometimes small problems can escalate, providing additional roadblocks that stand between the character and his or her goal.

The main character is usually, but not always, the viewpoint character—the character whose viewpoint is used to tell the story. The viewpoint character should be a doer, not an observer. This character is not a tour guide or a reporter taking down the facts. The viewpoint character guides the action and gets things done and is where the central conflict and change is focused.

Think about the character's world. It's what motivates, defines, and explains the character's actions. The character may be trying to escape it, get back to it, change it, or defend it from outside forces. It's sometimes said that every story is an escape story, with characters trying to escape—from their environment, from people around them, or from themselves.

Keep in mind that, for some scenes, it can be more interesting if the character doesn't know what is happening. This approach is often used in genres such as fantasy and mystery, but can be effective in other types of stories as well. A character's confusion can add drama, emotion, and realism (in the real world, we don't know what will happen next, and we sometimes find ourselves in situations that are bewildering until we figure out what's going on).

When you add secondary characters, consider contrast characters. Here's where you can have a little fun with quirky habits, out-of-the-ordinary personalities, or funny traits, as long as they are believable. Supporting characters help the viewpoint character find a solution to the problem, create conflict, or set the character on the wrong course. Avoid describing these characters at length when they are first introduced. Develop the characters through actions and dialogue, revealing a bit of information each time.

All characters need to serve a purpose; otherwise, there's no reason for them to take up space. Characters should each have their own world, even if it's never shown to the reader. That world is filled with friends, family, problems, opportunities, and desires. Pay attention to even the third or fourth character in your story. These subsidiary characters should have a role to play and a reason for being there. Either they figure into the plot, affect the dynamics of other character interactions, or create an action that alters the course of the story. Look carefully at each character and make sure he or she must be in the story.

Keep these secondary characters distinct and consistent. Provide all your characters with motivation. Remember Kurt Vonnegut's advice: "Every character should want something, even if it is only a glass of water." Turn those goals into actions. Make the character's responses show who the character is and what he is willing to do. The story may revolve around the main character's change, but secondary characters may change as well. Characters can and should evolve, but keep in mind that people do not make dramatic shifts within a short period of time without a life-changing event intervening.

Give your characters backstories, because how they speak and interact, what they know, how they dress, and how they react to various situations is the result of their backgrounds and experiences. For example, someone from an urban environment is used to sound, light, and activity. A country dweller is likely used to being near animals, having a quiet environment, and perhaps going to bed early. When my in-laws, who live in a city, stayed in my suburban home while I was away, they neglected to leave the porch light on and nearly couldn't find the house when they returned after dark. Their world is filled with streetlights, headlights, and other ambient light—they had no idea how dark a neighborhood can be in the absence of all that. Your characters' actions should reflect their backstories.

Create a worthy antagonist, not just a black-hat character. The antagonist should be a multifaceted character with his or her own desires, fears, and qualities, whether or not all are shown in the story. Remember that characters, like real people, have varied relationships. A villain may be evil to strangers but kind to his mother or younger sister. Characters can be revealed through their relationships and actions at work, within their family, and among strangers. Consider parent/child, sibling, romantic, platonic, abuser/victim, teacher/student, rival/adversary, friend, supervisor/employee, human/pet, and even person/God dynamics.

Characters' mannerisms, body language, facial expressions, speech, reactions, and even physical details should not be static. Real people are a combination of shifting traits expressed in various ways and affected by changes in circumstance and environment. A character should change over time and through experience, based on the events, surroundings, and other characters.

Even in the same span of time, a character should react differently depending on who is present. For example, a character's laugh when surrounded by friends in a lively bar may be unrestrained and raucous, but in a tense family situation, the same character may laugh in a caustic, even nasty way. Likewise, body language may become more guarded in a highly charged setting. Even a physical characteristic such as eyes will change with emotion.

Character is revealed in adversity. Throw in a few monkey wrenches. How a character approaches problems and makes choices gives readers a real sense of the character. Have the character experience failure. Create a critical turning point. Whatever happens, the situation must change. Your characters should not do something so far out of character that it's implausible, but characters shouldn't be too predictable either.

Sometimes, in short stories, characters have to serve multiple purposes. For example, if one character's purpose is to provide someone for the main character to show kindness toward and another character's purpose is to provide some comic relief in a dark scene, you may be able to have one character serve both those roles, as long as they don't contradict each other. If you find that you have too many characters in your story, consider combining them in ways that make sense.

Watch for default descriptions in your writing and don't just feed expectations (the nagging wife, the dad who doesn't know how to change a diaper, the crusty old neighbor). It is easy to fall back on clichés or your own stock phrases. Do your men often have "piercing blue" eyes and the women usually have "generous" mouths? Don't fill your stories with stereotypes or characters that look too much alike. Counter-stereotypes like female plumbers call attention to themselves. Make your characters as real and variable as the people you meet in the world.

Character Names

Bond. James Bond.

–Ian Fleming, *Dr. No*

Take the time to choose appropriate names for your characters. Make sure the names are easily distinguishable. Unless your characters are identical twins, avoid first names that begin with the same letter or that rhyme (Don and Dave, Mary and Carrie) and similar-sounding last names (Wilson and Tyson, for example) as they may confuse readers. Unusual ethnic names, unless required by the story, also add an unnecessary complication and can break the reader's concentration.

A wonderful name (Ebenezer Scrooge, Willy Wonka, Holly Golightly) can really help telegraph a character's essence, but a name is not a character. Don't think that if you give a character the name "Tex" your work is done. Differentiate your characters through dialogue and action as well as name.

Make sure your character names are appropriate to the character's age and time period. If you write a contemporary story and your young female characters have names such as Linda, Pat, and Donna, you are showing your age. Likewise, a grandmother is unlikely to have a name like Brianna or Kaylee. An excellent resource for name research is the Social Security Administration database of the most popular names by decade. It's accessible on their website: ssa.gov/oact/babynames/decades.

Note that given names are not the only things that have changed over the years. Names for roles are also different. For example, fifty years ago, teachers were known by their last names as "Miss [last name]," but today's teachers are usually known to students as "Miss [first name]" or even just by their first name. Modern grandmas are more likely to be "Mom-Mom," "Momo," or "Mima." Go back a generation or two, and it's more likely to be "Grandma [last name]," "Granny," or "Grandmother." Grandparents in French, Italian, or German families might be called "Mami," "Nonna," or

"Oma." Do your research so the terms you use will ring true.

Life (at least life in the United States) has gotten more casual. People don't wait to be introduced, and complete strangers feel comfortable using a person's first name. This can vary by geographic region, age, cultural background, and social status. Older people are often not as comfortable with familiarity and may use a more formal manner. My mother, when asked by a hairdresser for her name, provided her last name. When the hairdresser said, "No, I meant your first name," my mother responded, "Mrs."

If you are writing fiction, do not use names of real people unless you enjoy spending time with lawyers. It's just not worth the grief. What you think is a flattering reference could well annoy, anger, or enrage the person concerned. There are ways you can include public figures, but be extremely careful and read up on what is allowable and what is not. If you are unsure, consult an attorney, or you may find yourself not only sued, but sued by someone with extraordinarily deep pockets.

Character tags are a way to identify a character by a trait or physical characteristic. They are more than just random quirks; they tell the reader something about the character. In old movies, the guys in the white hats were the "good" cowboys and guys in the black hats were the "bad" cowboys. More subtle tags might be a strong handshake to indicate confidence, or frequent combing of hair to show vanity.

Names can serve as character tags in an obvious way by referring directly to a trait ("Big Bob," "Pudge," "Red") or in a more subtle way by using a name that creates a mental picture ("Grover," "Priscilla," "Tiffany"). The best tags help convey not only visual traits but also the character's personality or habits. Character tags can help create tension between characters and can make characters memorable and more real for the reader.

Character tags can be drawn from gestures, physical appearance, voice, mental state, scent, verbal tic, body language, or other aspects of the character's look or behavior. They help readers tell one character from another and telegraph information important to the story. Characters can have multiple tags and may have positive and negative tags. The tags must be repeated (sparingly), in slightly different ways, to be memorable without being obvious.

Character tags can create suspense (an out-of-place scent), provide foreshadowing (a cough), or add humor (an odd habit or manner of speech). The description of the tag can shade its meaning. "Slim" might be "slim as the stem of a champagne flute" or "slim as a desiccated mummy." If one character only sees another character's positive (or negative) tags, the result can be misunderstanding, which can contribute to the conflict in the story.

Character tags can also serve as a way to reference a character that is not named. For example, if the main character sees a suspicious stranger, and you want to reference that stranger (perhaps he will be seen again in another location), you will need a memorable way to refer to him. Since your character wouldn't know the person's name, you can refer to the stranger as "Plaid Pants," "Mustache Man," or some other tag that identifies him.

Attributes/Descriptions

> The best modern fiction and nonfiction writers let a character's visible persona speak for itself. They carefully choose a few details that hint at the underlying character. Through the choice of detail, they lead readers to certain inevitable conclusions about the character they are describing.
>
> –Jack Hart, "Building Character: What the Fiction Writers Say"

Don't make characters one-dimensional. People are seldom characterized by one trait, and even those who are strongly defined by a single trait will not always be consistent. You may know someone who is kind, but a kind person can also be a bigot, have a drug habit, or get road rage. And then there are people who are kind when others are watching, and kick the dog when no one is looking.

Resist the urge to immediately tell readers everything about the character. Readers appreciate enough information to allow them to visualize the character, but they don't need to know every physical detail, every character trait, and every bit of the character's backstory the moment the character is introduced. Give the reader a few details that provide a general idea of the age, sex, and background of the character, but use actions and dialogue to show whether the character is neat or tidy, rich or poor, happy or sad.

Giving the reader too much information up front not only makes the story less interesting, but also deprives the reader of the joy of discovery and limits your own ability to let the character emerge and change over time. In real life, when you meet someone new, you form an impression based on the limited information you are given ("This is Gary. He has a child in my daughter's preschool."). Your impression will change over time as you learn new information ("He's a stay-at-home dad."), and you may even make mistaken assumptions ("His husband, Bill, is a consultant who travels extensively."). Let readers have the same opportunity to discover characters for themselves, get to know them, and form their own judgements or mistaken assumptions about them. Allow the backstory to emerge as unobtrusively as possible.

You can tick off a list of attributes and physical details to describe a character, but there are other, better ways to bring characters to life. You can do any of the following:

- Provide details or quirks that show individuality.
- Show the environment that surrounds the character, particularly the surroundings the character has chosen for himself or herself.
- Let the character show us who he or she is through unspoken thoughts.
- Put the character into action—show us what the character does and how, from small mannerisms to heroic (or evil) actions.
- Show how the character reacts to other people.
- Show how other people react to the character.
- Let the character talk and thereby show us who he or she is with dialogue, manner of speech, vocabulary, and expressions.

Worry more about personality traits than physical descriptions. Be consistent, except to show logical, meaningful change in the character through the story. There should be some motivation for the change (to make it plausible). Show traits, don't just tell us about them. Use actions, reactions, and interactions and convey them with hints (how others react to the character and what the character says and does).

Here is a relatively simple, yet brilliant, description that Philip Roth used to describe a character in his short story, "The Conversion of the Jews": "His mother was a round, tired, gray-haired penguin of a woman whose gray skin had begun to feel the tug of gravity and the weight of her own history." The description is short and the vocabulary is probably no more than second-grade level, but this single sentence tells us everything we need to know about the character's mother.

Be true to the character. If the character is a child, research the vocabulary, mannerisms, interests, and activities of children that age. If it's a contemporary story, don't have the child playing with toys or reading stories from your childhood. Use current playthings. Today's children have cell phones, iPads, and other electronic gadgets. If your character is a high school dropout who lives in an urban setting, don't have her quoting Thoreau, unless it's explained and there's a reason for it.

Why should we care? What makes your characters tick? How do they analyze information, form strategies, solve problems? What are they afraid of? Proud of? Willing to fight for? Each character should have something at stake. Characters reveal themselves through actions. How a character reacts under stress, makes decisions, and solves problems should tell the reader something.

Think about how you can convey traits such as impatience, laziness, generosity, or fastidiousness without using adjectives. A quirky habit, a repeated gesture, or a dialogue idiosyncrasy can make a character memorable and tell the reader something about the character. Someone who frequently checks the locks may be fearful, while someone who doesn't bother with a seatbelt is likely to be a risk taker. Traits can also be misunderstood, which can provide tension, especially if the reader senses that the character is different from what he or she appears to be.

Unspoken thoughts can be extremely helpful in revealing traits such as impulsivity, anxiety, optimism, and obsession. Louise Boggess says, "Thoughts form the hotline to the reader, so the reader must see the viewpoint character weigh the decisions, react to the other characters, and argue the right or wrong choice of action, keeping the inner conflict rising."

Examine the motivations for your characters. Are their actions plausible, given the background information you've provided? Make sure their actions are "in character" unless they are obviously pushing themselves beyond the usual for a reason. For example, a character with a poor self-concept who is often ill at ease would not be able to give a speech without suffering some degree of distress unless you provide an explanation (they've been taking lessons, getting therapy, or taking medication).

How a character perceives details can be revealing. A character who is shallow and materialistic may notice someone's jewelry, brand of car, and style of clothing; a character who is interested in world problems would more likely notice bumper stickers, evidence of conspicuous consumption, and whether the lawn sprinkler was left running. One character might notice an interesting wallpaper pattern while another is focused on the music playing in the background or aromas coming from the kitchen.

Because you want your reader to be able to identify with, or at least sympathize with, the main character, the character should be somewhat likeable, but don't make the main character unrealistic. No one is free from flaws. Clayton C. Barbeau urges writers to "watch for warts." Warts (negative traits) are what make people unique. Barbeau gets his wart analogy from Chaucer's description of a character in the *Canterbury Tales* who was distinguished by a hair-sprouting wart on the end of his nose. Distinguishing characteristics don't have to be warts, but if none of your characters have any warts, Barbeau recommends going back and adding some so that your characters seem more like living people than puppets.

The negative traits shouldn't be so off-putting as to make readers lose interest in what happens to the character. Negative characteristics such as untidiness, awkwardness, tardiness, and unstylishness, unless extreme, can be accepted, and even found endearing. Characteristics such as bigotry, meanness, stupidity, and violent tendencies are much more difficult to make sympathetic, but can add complexity to a character. There are also flaws that nearly everyone can identify with such as being klutzy, forgetful, or socially awkward. Universal feelings can also elicit empathy. Feeling underqualified or unprepared, embarrassed, frustrated, jealous, impatient, or anxious are emotional states everyone has experienced.

Watch how you portray men and women in your stories. If you decide to change the gender of a secondary character, don't just take a male character and make it female, or vice versa. If your characters are interchangeable, they are not fully developed (Are the men and women you know all the same?).

If you have difficulty writing characters of the opposite gender, ask for feedback. Women are not set decoration, and they are more than just a description (perky little blonde); they have minds, motivations, and experiences that drive them. Write women as human beings—complex, multifaceted individuals, not just companions, wives, love interests, conquests, victims, or foils for the male characters. They should be full participants in the story.

Women talk to each other. Create opportunities for your female characters to talk to each other, preferably about something other than men. Avoid common female character clichés such as the slut/other woman who pays for it in the end, the evil seductress who leads the hero astray, the shy librarian who needs a man to help her uncover her desires, the "one of the guys" girl, and the iconic mother figure (baking brownies and diapering babies).

Consider racial, gender, and sexual orientation diversity. African-American women are not always sassy, and Asian men are not all shy electronics wizards. A gay man is as likely to be an executive as an interior designer, and a lesbian may be a beautiful blonde. Keep in mind that it is increasingly common for people who identify as bisexual, gay, transgender, or transsexual to be open about it. Kate Elliott advises writers to "assume every character you write is a full human being just as you take yourself to be, with no more or less mystery than you feel for your own self."

Character Checklist

❒ Have you carefully chosen the characters, including a viewpoint character, for your story?

❒ Have you selected names that fit the characters and that are easy for the reader to distinguish?

❒ Is your main character a flawed person whom readers will be able to identify with?

❒ Are your characters—even the secondary characters—multidimensional?

❒ Have you conveyed character attributes and descriptions through unspoken thoughts and actions?

❒ Are all of the characters necessary (do they serve different purposes)?

❒ Have you provided the characters with motivation?

❒ Have you avoided stereotypes and clichés?

Telling the Story

Point of View

> It's harder to write in the third person but the advantage is you move around better.
>
> –Ernest Hemingway

Choose your point of view carefully. Point of view affects the way the story is told, the facts the reader is privy to, and the internal thoughts conveyed. The story is being told through a narrator, but you need to choose whether the narrator is a character in the story (the main character or a secondary character), someone observing the story, or you, the writer.

With first person ("I," "we," "my"), the author is telling the story or is telling the story as one of the characters: "As I stood on the course, mallet in hand and enjoying the smell of cut grass and the flickering of the fireflies, I began to reconsider whether or not cocktail croquet was indeed 'a tradition'" (from "Cocktail Croquet" by Rich Barnett, *The Beach House*). In first-person point of view, you are in one head and can create and maintain a distinct inner voice (think Bridget Jones). You are limited to experiences, perceptions, and conversations that can be seen or be sensed by the narrator, but you can choose whether or not to be a trustworthy source of information.

Use the first person if it's important that the reader know the thoughts and feelings of your character and if that knowledge is essential for setting up the conflict. Use it if the events of the story are best revealed through the eyes of the character and if the character is best revealed by telling the story from his or her viewpoint.

Remember that if you choose the first-person narrator, that character has to be present in every scene in order to be able to relate it to the reader. There are devices you can use to insert information about events outside the narrator's sphere, for example reading about events in someone's diary or in a newspaper, overhearing an event, or having another character describe the event to the narrator, but if you find yourself falling back on this more than once or twice, you may want to reconsider the first-person narrator.

Even within a first-person point of view, there are some decisions to be made. Consider this short scene, as told by three different first-person narrators:

> 1. I eased in next to the blonde at the bar and looked into her inviting eyes. "Are you my destiny?" I asked.
>
> 2. I see it almost every night in this bar. Balding, the far side of fifty, pizza waistline and beer breath, but supremely confident that the gorgeous blonde will fall for his tired line.
>
> 3. I chuckled into my beer as the bail-jumper we'd been searching for for two weeks sat down at the bar, right next to my best fugitive recovery agent.

Note the differences in perception, access to the facts of the situation, and tone. First-person present tense can be difficult to maintain, but does provide a sense of intimacy and immediacy. The reader really gets to know the character. Best of all, *the writer* really gets to know the character. Some writers find that once they get into the role, they find the character's voice and can just run with it.

The first-person narrator doesn't have to tell all. You can withhold information. The narrator can be evasive, can lie to other characters, and can lie by omission to the reader. A famous example is *The Murder of Roger Ackroyd* by Agatha Christie. The mystery is narrated by a character who (spoiler alert) turns out to be the murderer. The book, which was published in 1926, caused quite a stir and set the stage for the concept of the "unreliable narrator," a term coined by Wayne C. Booth in *The Rhetoric of Fiction* in 1961. Unreliable narrators may be insane, liars, or too young or impaired to report information accurately. If you choose to use an unreliable narrator, play fair and give the reader some hints to avoid having readers feel tricked.

When writing in the first person from a character's point of view, you will have to find ways to get that character's description into the story. Avoid the hackneyed look in the mirror and instead use the reactions of other characters ("Were you always a blonde?"), unspoken thoughts ("I'll never get down to 140 pounds this way."), or actions ("I coated my freckled arms with sunblock.").

The biggest advantage of first-person point of view is that it puts the reader in the story and in the thick of the action. It is an immediate, eyewitness account that is highly subjective but real. The biggest drawback is that it is sometimes limiting to not have the benefit of seeing and being able to report on all pertinent events in the story. The narrator also has to be alive at the end of the story (think about it). If a character in the story dies, have someone who is alive to tell the tale be the narrator. One last caution: If you write in first person, make sure you don't default to your own feelings and voice. The "I" in the story should be the *character*, not *you*.

Second-person point of view ("you") is less common, and can be effective in the right story, but is tricky to pull off successfully. The story focuses on the reader: "You wish that you'd kept that Keurig coffeemaker you got as a wedding present, but since it came from Josh's sister, it seemed only right to give it back. No wedding, no Keurig. But after consuming so much alcohol last night, you're desperate for caffeine to lighten the pounding headache" ("Why You Trashed Vera Wang" from *Sandy Shorts* by Nancy Powichroski Sherman). Second person can give an offbeat, eccentric tone to the story. You speak directly to the reader, and the reader becomes a character in the story.

In third-person point of view ("he," "she," "they"), the narrator tells the story: "Nora hadn't been back to the beach or the boardwalk since that day, but had so often relived every detail that it was as if it were permanently etched in her mind" ("Untethered" by Margaret Farrell Kirby, from *The Boardwalk*). In the third-person point of view, the narrator tells the story and can be privy to all actions, conversations, and events in the story. The third person is telling the story from an observer's point of view, which can put the reader at a distance.

A third-person narrator is observing from the outside and so is not part of the action. Like an invisible reporter, the third person follows the action, moving from one key scene to the next, always at the right place at the right time. The third-person narrator can have access to all of the characters' backstories, actions, and even thoughts. Within third person, you can choose an omniscient narrator (the author can enter the mind of any character) or limited point of view (author enters the mind of only one character).

The omniscient third person can provide contrasting points of view and offers the opportunity to switch characters (which can be useful in a novel but can be difficult to carry off within the confines of a short story). If you choose this approach, be careful to alert the reader if you change the perspective to another character. For a short story, you may want to limit yourself to one character's point of view.

In the limited third-person point of view, the narrator observes all but enters the head of only one character. An example of this is, "Allie tossed her hair back, ignoring the nagging feeling that Steve distrusted her. She couldn't bear to think he suspected her." The third person is clear ("she"), but a bystander would have no idea that she had a "nagging feeling" or that she thought Steve might suspect her. The narrator (Allie's point of view) can only speculate about what Steve is thinking. Use third person if using first person limits your ability to demonstrate the weaknesses of the main character, or if the story needs to be told objectively.

You may want to experiment with telling the story from different points of view or from different characters' points of view.

Whatever you choose, you should be consistent, as it can be confusing to readers when the point of view jumps around. If you decide to tell the story from different points of view, make sure there is an obvious break at each change.

The Viewpoint Character

> **A story about everyone is a story about no one.**
>
> –Beth Hill, "Viewpoint Character and the Need to Choose Wisely"

The character you use to tell the story through is called the viewpoint character or point of view (POV) character. The viewpoint character carries the author's message to the reader, which may be a universal truth, and is the character who is affected by what is won or lost in the story. The way the character experiences these events and how the character responds, reacts, and changes is usually at the heart of the story.

The viewpoint character is not just the focus of the action; the viewpoint character is the emotional focus of the story. That doesn't mean that the viewpoint character is necessarily the most important character or even the most interesting. Consider *The Great Gatsby*. The main focus is on the mysterious millionaire, Jay Gatsby, but the story is actually told by Nick Carraway, who provides the viewpoint for the story.

When choosing the viewpoint, consider the character who has access to just enough facts and events to tell the story, while leaving a little to the imagination, a character who has an interesting backstory or manner, a character who has a big part of the story, and a character whom the reader will enjoy riding shotgun with. With a single viewpoint character, the story can still be told in first-, second-, or third-person point of view.

Establish the point of view and whose head you are inside immediately, so readers know who is telling the story. Reveal the character's thoughts and feelings so the reader gets into the character quickly. How other characters react to the main character adds dimension and helps reveal character history (backstory).

Make sure that the viewpoint doesn't wander around like a lost dog looking for a handout:

> Mary looked at her husband, Steve, and shivered. She wondered if his lie meant that he was having an affair. *She fell for it,* Steve thought to himself as Little Eric gazed at his parents and considered how lucky he was to have parents who were still in love.

This sort of "head hopping" (jumping from one character's thoughts to another's) is disconcerting and confusing to readers.

Some authors like to provide multiple viewpoints, which can be a way of including different observations or even conflicting versions of the same event. In novels, the point of view can change with each chapter. A short story rarely provides enough real estate for the back and forth required for multiple viewpoints to be effective. Jumping around from one character to another in a narrow space can dilute the intensity of the story, confuse the reader, and diminish the author's authority. The narrative can seem arbitrary rather than controlled, and the reader is left adrift, with no real connection to or investment in the story. For beginning writers, a single viewpoint character is more manageable and less likely to lead to problems.

It is possible to write a story with a narrator who is not a character (the narrator is an unseen bystander), but bystanders have no emotional involvement and therefore provide no reason for the reader to care. Stories narrated from a bystander point of view tend to read more like a police blotter than a story. Readers want to know what at least one of the characters thinks and feels.

One exception to this is the "implied narrator." Using this approach, the author tells the story, but as an unidentified informed viewer. The story is told in the third person, but the narrator has knowledge of the setting and characters, and the reader gets a sense of the narrator's emotions and thoughts. While this approach allows the author to make an emotional connection, it may be difficult to really tell the story effectively without being able to get into the heads of any of the characters involved.

Consider the market when choosing the viewpoint. If your intended target is a magazine read primarily by young women, you may not want to use an older man as the viewpoint character, unless it's to make a point. Children's book and magazine publishers want a child's point of view to dominate rather than an adult's so their readers can identify with the character. If you are writing a romance novel for women, you will want to have a female viewpoint. If you are writing a romance novel for an LGBT audience, you will want a viewpoint character who is the same sex as the romantic target.

Viewpoint is particularly tricky in mysteries. To create suspense, some facts must be withheld and some red herrings introduced, but the reader can't be made to feel cheated or lied to. If the viewpoint character knows too much, you may have to either switch the viewpoint to another character or find a way to legitimately withhold or obfuscate.

Just remember that your narrator can't provide information he or she doesn't have access to or give insights based on events the narrator wasn't present to see. The narrator can't observe things out of his or her field of vision (the back of his own head, for example) and can't describe things that an individual isn't able to describe (what he looks like asleep, his own death). The narrator is not privy to conversations, events, and activities he or she has not observed or heard about from other characters and can speculate, but not know, the unspoken thoughts and emotions of the other characters. Whatever you choose for your viewpoint, be consistent unless there is a reason to change point of view or tense, and even then you should be consistent within the scene.

Voice

> **When you are trying to find your writing voice don't try to emulate any writer, not even your favorite. Sit quietly, listen, listen again, then listen some more and write out everything the voice says with no censoring—none—not one word.**
>
> –Jan Marquart, *The Basket Weaver*

Voice is one of those things that is difficult to explain, but you know it when you see it. From a technical standpoint, it is a combination of vocabulary, content, theme, rhythm, and style of writing, but the combination creates an effect that can distinguish one writer's work from another as clearly as one painter's work from another. Think about some of the authors you have read and consider how different James Joyce is from James Patterson, and Jack London is from Jack Kerouac.

It has to do with writing *style*, but that is not the same thing as *voice*. Style concerns sentence structure, use of metaphors and imagery, and the formality or informality of the writing itself. Voice is affected by regional, cultural, ethnic, and religious heritage; educational level and life experience; books, films, and other cultural experiences; and manner of speech (cadence, word choice, and rhythm). Voice is the special sauce an accomplished writer uses to give his writing added flavor and distinction.

A writer's voice can vary, depending on the work, especially if the writer works in different genres or under several pen names. Content affects voice to the extent that an informal, confessional sort of voice might lend itself well to a "chicklit" novel, but not so much to an academic biography. An expansive, narrative voice might lend itself well to a family saga but not to a noir short story. Writers may change voice when writing for different ages, audiences, and markets.

Voice is what makes you different from other writers. It's not only your choice of words and the way you put those words together, but also the way you see the world, your sensibility and outlook, your original take on things, and the "feel" of the writing that conveys a sense of your nature and creates a distinct persona. Developing a personal voice is something many writers struggle with, but, like personal style, it is more authentic when it emerges on its own rather than when it is intentionally constructed.

Telling the Story Checklist

❒ Have you chosen the best way to tell the story (first, second, or third person)?

❒ Is the viewpoint character the one most appropriate for telling the story?

❒ If you are in one character's head, are you conveying only things that character could know?

❒ Have you avoided "head hopping"?

❒ Have you shown the character's emotions and not just told readers about them?

❒ Is the "I" character different from you?

❒ Is your character's voice consistent with his or her education, background, location, intelligence, and age?

Dialogue

Creating Realistic Dialogue

Dialogue is not conversation; it is an exchange of dramatic action.

–Shelly Lowenkopf, *The Fiction Writer's Handbook*

Unless your audience is a group of five-year-olds who will sit still and listen while someone tells them a tale, your story should be more than one long narrative—it should have characters talking. In other words, *dialogue*. Dialogue is a way of showing conflict, revealing character traits, and drawing the reader into the story. What characters say and how they say it is key to a winning story. Dialogue should move the story forward, show something about the character, convey information, or some combination of these.

Dialogue is what brings a story to life. Without dialogue, the story will be flat and seem more like a report than a story. There will be a wall between the reader and the action—almost literally. Readers will see large squares of uninterrupted text, looming like impenetrable roadblocks, rather than short bursts of inviting dialogue that tempt the reader to jump right in. Dialogue lets the reader take part in the action by watching the characters interact.

Dialogue is how we learn about the characters—how they think, react, behave, and speak. How characters talk provides tremendous insights into the characters' backgrounds and personalities. You can describe a person in detail, but once that person opens his or her mouth and speaks, you really start to get a sense of what he or she is all about. What the character chooses to say (or not say), the words used, the manner of speech, the body language that accompanies the words, and the way the words are spoken all contribute to conveying a character's essence.

Does a story *have* to have dialogue? Technically, no, but if you are asking because writing dialogue scares you, give it a try. Your story will likely be much better for it, and you will have more "showing" and less "telling." Stories without dialogue are often just rambling narratives, not stories.

Keep dialogue short and punchy (unless the character is a windbag or someone who likes to give speeches). Natural-sounding dialogue has contractions, sentence fragments, incomplete thoughts, slang, and even poor grammar. Spoken language is less formal than written language, and each person doesn't say much at one time (except in Shakespeare).

Read dialogue aloud to make sure it sounds realistic. In real life, people interrupt each other, question, pause, and react. They may cry, laugh, sneeze, hiccup, or choke up. Dialogue shouldn't just be people talking at each other, and it shouldn't just be a way to inject information.

Convey setting in dialogue, but be careful with ethnic, regional, or cultural dialects and accents (unless you're Mark Twain, and even he got into trouble). Drop a hint here and there (enough to let readers "hear" the voice), but don't make readers slog through a dialect that is difficult to pronounce and read. A strategic "y'all" easily communicates a Southern speaker without forcing readers through a barrage of slang and alternate spellings to indicate the accent. This is also true of foreign terms. Toss a few in every now and then to help convey the setting or a character's nationality, but don't have readers running to Google Translate in the middle of your story.

Do use phrases that convey local knowledge. For example, for people on Long Island, it isn't New York, it's "the city." Say you're going into "the city" and everyone knows what you mean (because there *is* no other city to Long Islanders). If you have a Midwesterner order a soft drink, it should probably be "pop."

Once you complete a section of dialogue, take a close look at your dialogue tags—the explanations tacked onto the ends of dialogue ("he said," "she whispered"). Dialogue tags tell the reader who is speaking and are necessary only when it isn't clear who is talking. A rule of thumb is that if the reader has no idea who might be speaking, start with the speaker's name (Mary said, "Eat your breakfast."). If the reader has a pretty good idea who is speaking, put the tag at the end ("Eat your breakfast," Mary said.). And if the reader knows who is speaking, don't use a dialogue tag ("Eat your breakfast.").

Some writers search for exotic substitutes to avoid having to use "said" over and over. What they don't realize is that readers are so used to seeing "he said" and "she said" that those dialogue tags are nearly invisible. Once you start plugging in a string of "he trumpeted," "she bellowed," and the like, the dialogue tags call attention to themselves and become a distraction. In many cases, careful wording and paragraphing will limit the need to use tags at all, but where they are needed to avoid confusion, stick to "said" or simple substitutes such as "replied" or "answered."

Rare use of terms such as "whispered," "yelled," or "shouted" is also acceptable. Just remember that dialogue tags must be vocalizations—ways of speaking (shrieked, murmured, explained). Don't make mistakes like these: "'I bet not,' he laughed." "'Not today,' she frowned." You can't laugh or frown words. Here are a couple of options for correcting these errors: "'I bet not,' he said, laughing." "'Not today,' she said with a frown."

Use bits of physical movement to augment the dialogue and control the pace. Actions such as rubbing eyes, putting glasses on, opening a drawer, or closing a purse, are sometimes called "beats." They interrupt the dialogue, so they should be used sparingly, but they can help bring the setting and scene to life. Beats also allow you to direct the reader's attention and can provide a necessary pause so the reader can absorb information or appreciate what is transpiring. Resist the urge to describe every action, but provide some hints so readers can imagine the scene.

You can dramatically alter the meaning of dialogue by injecting a well-chosen action. Watch how this line of dialogue changes:

> "I do love you," Matt said, dabbing his eyes with a tissue.

> "I do love you," Matt said, stifling a yawn.
>
> "I do love you," Matt said, taking her hand.
>
> "I do love you," Matt said, wiping his nose on his sleeve.

Within a scene, be consistent with how you refer to characters. If you have "Sarah said" in one part of the scene and then "Mrs. Cameron" in another, readers may become confused unless you've made the connection. How the character is referenced also depends on the point of view. If the scene is being told from Sarah Cameron's daughter's point of view, "her mother said" would be a more appropriate attribution.

You don't need to explain dialogue to your readers. Sentences like this: "'So that's it,' he said in astonishment," detract from the drama of the story. Beginning writers often feel the need to tack an adverb onto each bit of dialogue ("'Is that you?' he asked hopefully." "'Yes,' she answered eagerly."). This practice can actually be entertaining in the right context, as was proven by the Tom Swift books. Here are a few Tom Swifties to demonstrate:

> "Where's Ruth?" Tom asked ruthlessly.
>
> "They had to amputate them both at the ankles," Tom said defeatedly.
>
> "I unclogged the drain with a vacuum cleaner," Tom said succinctly.

If you find yourself using an adverb with dialogue, check to see whether any explanation is necessary. If it is, try constructing the dialogue to convey the action. Instead of "he said angrily" use "he shouted." Or better yet, work action into the dialogue: "'I've had it,' he said, banging his fist on the desk." And make sure that the dialogue actually reflects the emotion. "I don't think so" doesn't convey anger, but "How dare you!" would eliminate the need for "she said angrily."

Dialogue among Characters

> The full dialogue pattern consists of three distinct parts: who speaks, what he says, and how he says it. Remember these key words: see, hear, and react.
>
> –Louise Boggess, *How to Write Short Stories That Sell*

Each character should speak differently, and they shouldn't all sound like you. Speech reflects age, cultural background, geography, education, occupation, gender, social standing, and personality. The best dialogue can be read with no tags, and the reader still knows who said what. If you use a character dialogue quirk, which can be an excellent way to add authenticity, don't overdo it. A teenager may say "awesome" all the time, but put it in every bit of dialogue and your readers will want to choke you.

If you have fully developed the characters in your own mind, you may find you can put them in a situation, start the ball rolling, and then begin to feel as if you are copying down what they say. If a character "says" something unexpected, see how it plays out. Don't edit dialogue as you are writing it. Step back, watch the characters interact, and write down what comes to mind. Later, during editing, you can take out unnecessary material, tighten the sentences, and make certain the scene is believable, in the proper point of view, and that it accomplishes what you wanted it to (presumably move the story forward in some way).

No one talks the same way all of the time, and neither should your characters. Notice how people you know talk differently to different people. For example, most men clean up their language around women, older people, and in job settings when around superiors. A teenage girl would likely talk to her mother in a different way than she would talk to her brother, a teacher, a girlfriend, or a boy she likes. Keep this in mind when using dialogue. Your characters' speech will change, based on the situation, people present, frame of mind, mood, and other factors.

Use dialogue to convey information (location, weather, and

characters' appearances) in short, vivid bursts rather than long, adjective-packed narratives. Use actions ("He stamped the floor to shake the snow off his large, half-frozen feet.") rather than sticking in explanatory text that reads like a weather report. Dialogue should be things people really might say, not just a way for the author to inject information. You often see this sort of fact-packed dialogue on television shows: ("That syringe looks like it contains Byetta, a medication for diabetes that was originally derived from a compound found in the saliva of the Gila monster."). You should also never have a character tell another character something he or she would already know just as a way of getting the information on the page.

Dialogue isn't just *what* is said, it's *how* it's said. The type of speech should reflect the character. Choppy or smooth sentences, correct or incorrect grammar, spelling indicating an accent or dialect, expression, mannerisms, and the formality or informality of the tone give clues to the character's background. Incorporate differences in speech due to age, occupation, education, environment, and mood, and remember that responses don't always have to be verbal; they can be facial expressions, gestures, body language, and movements. A character can answer with a shrug or a smile, or might just turn and walk away. Having characters ignore questions, misunderstand questions, or provide a politician's response (an answer to a different question) can add realism to dialogue.

Make sure your characters are actually interacting. Dialogue without real engagement is like actors doing a script reading. It seems artificial because it is. How often do people just speak to each other back and forth without something else going on? In real life, people move, touch each other, and interact with their surroundings while they are talking. They are walking, looking at their phones, picking up and putting down objects, handing each other things, looking at each other (or not), and otherwise in motion. People may be interrupted (by a phone call or another person entering the room), lose their train of thought, change the subject, or suddenly remember something. Incorporate actions like these with dialogue to add realism to your writing.

Dialogue doesn't always have to be talking on the move, like a *Law & Order* episode, but talking heads aren't interesting, and people do talk as they are standing up, sitting down, waiting in lines, going in and out of buildings, driving, getting in and out of cars, and (unfortunately) eating.

Actual dialogue is wordy, repetitive, and punctuated with "uh," "like," "you know," and other verbal tics. In real life, dialogue often contains meaningless exchanges such as, "Hi, how are you?" "Fine, how are you?" While this is realistic, no one wants to waste time reading that. Skip right to dialogue that tells us something about the characters or the situation.

Use fragments, unanswered questions, evasive replies, abrupt changes of topic, interruptions, and one- and two-word responses. You can include clichés and grammatical mistakes or an "uh" here or there if it fits the character, but readers will tire quickly if you overdo it. Verbal tics that are ignored in spoken language call attention to themselves when written on the page.

Make sure dialogue contains some conflict. People discussing what cereal to have for breakfast isn't interesting, unless there's a reason for tension (is it an abusive situation and the man's dialogue has a threatening edge to it?). Tap into emotion. Use body language, facial expressions, and nonspeech vocalizations such as yawns, coughs, chuckles, and sighs to amplify dialogue.

It can be particularly effective to show conflicting emotions. One character might be increasingly angry, while the other remains calm or even smiles or laughs. This can reveal character traits and personalities but can also offer insights into relationships. For example, a couple might be arguing, and one becomes angry quickly, while the other is a step or two behind.

Where appropriate (viewpoint characters only), include some unspoken thoughts. This can be done by breaking up blocks of dialogue like this: "'I'm calling her now,' Bob said. *What a mess.* 'We have to decide sooner or later.'" You can also break up dialogue with bits of narration: "'I'm calling her now,' Bob said. It had been three weeks since he'd raised the issue with Sarah. 'We have to decide sooner or later.'"

Make sure that the dialogue is appropriate to the speaker. Listen for snippets of interesting dialogue in public places such as restaurants and malls, and record them for future stories. It can be especially helpful to listen to the speech of people close to the age, sex, background, and occupation of your character. Compare these expressions, which all convey roughly the same sentiment but indicate different ages and backgrounds: "Is this true?" "Are you kidding me?" "You yankin' my chain?" "Seriously?" "WTF?"

When you write dialogue, give each speaker his or her own paragraph, even if the paragraph is a single word:

> "Jared, I think we have a communication problem. I tell you how I feel and you don't seem to pay attention. I pour my heart out to you. Can't you at least give me a meaningful response?"
>
> "What?"

The paragraph should include any dialogue tags, descriptions of action, and unspoken thoughts relating to that character:

> Holly dried her eyes with the back of her sleeve. "It's like you're not even listening," she said, as she saw him turn toward her. *At least he looks concerned now.* "Do you still love me?
>
> "Any idea where the remote is?" Jared asked.

Dialogue can also be used to smooth transitions. You usually want to get characters from one place to another (or from one scene to the next) as quickly as possible. With dialogue, a single sentence can transport the character ("He waved goodbye and headed for the train.").

Unspoken Thoughts

> **Most fiction is character driven, and I'm convinced that readers' most-loved fiction is that which allows us to delve into the innermost thoughts of its characters, in the process finding moments of recognition—the chance to recognize ourselves in fictional characters and identify with them on multiple levels—and discovering more about ourselves.**
>
> –Arlene Prunkl, "Dialogue in Fiction: Part V—Writing Your Characters' Thoughts"

Unspoken thoughts (sometimes called "internal monologue") can be a powerful way to convey a character's personality, background, and attitude. By allowing your reader to see what your character is thinking, you create an intimate connection.

Whenever you provide the thoughts going on in a character's head, remember to keep the thoughts in the same voice (vocabulary, style of speech, and manner) as the character's spoken dialogue. Unspoken thoughts are confidences that tell the reader about the character and his or her goals, dreams, worries, problems, and needs. These thoughts should embellish and enhance dialogue, not duplicate it.

Unspoken thoughts are usually differentiated by italic type, not quotation marks (which indicate spoken words). If the thoughts are simply being described, no differentiation is required.

> Unspoken thoughts: *Not again.* She couldn't believe the guy was back.
>
> Described thoughts: She had wondered whether he was going to come back again, and now here he was.
>
> Unspoken thoughts: *In my dreams.*
>
> Described thoughts: It occurred to him that this would only happen in his dreams.

It can be particularly effective to have a character speak one thing but be thinking something different: "'Nice to meet you, too.'

OK, I'll play along. She obviously hadn't told her husband about us." This intensifies tension and can be a way to show a character struggling with a problem or being dishonest to another character. It can also be a way of sharing facts with the reader that are being withheld from one or more of the characters.

Remember that, even in their thoughts, characters cannot have knowledge of events that happened outside their experience unless another character has told them about it. They can wonder, speculate, or guess, but they cannot appear to have observed characters in a scene where they were not present.

Unspoken thoughts should be seamless within the scene and any spoken dialogue and be unobtrusive. Save this technique for times when the character's thoughts are revealing, essential to the story, and natural in the context of the character and the scene. Don't waste it on a character thinking about an upcoming dentist appointment or deciding which brand of deodorant to buy.

Dialogue Checklist

❒ Have you used dialogue, where possible, instead of narration?

❒ Does the dialogue seem like a real conversation (it doesn't sound stilted or unnatural)?

❒ Are your dialogue tags necessary and unobtrusive?

❒ Are all the dialogue tags vocalizations?

❒ Do the characters sound different from each other, reflecting different backgrounds, education, and personalities?

❒ Have you combined dialogue with action where possible?

❒ Does the dialogue advance the story or reveal information?

❒ Have you resisted the urge to explain dialogue?

The Title

Don't let your titles be flimsy, weak things. Give them bones. A spine. Give them purpose. Anchor the title to the work. To *your* work. Your book is special. Give it a special title.

–Chuck Wendig, "Choosing the Right Title for Your Work"

Which book would people be more likely to buy?

Inspirational Stories and Anecdotes
or
Chicken Soup for the Soul

The right title can mean the difference between rejection or becoming a marketing phenomenon. Giving your story a bland, generic title is missing an opportunity to make your story stand out. Consider this: The original title for *Of Mice and Men* was *Something That Happened.* It would still have been an exceptional book, but it is certainly a more memorable book with that intriguing title.

The title affects how a story is perceived (by editors, agents, judges, and of course readers) and whether or not the story is even read. For that reason, the title (whether it's for a book or a short story) is a critical part of the work and one worth spending some time thinking about.

Editors, agents, and contest judges are impressed with a well-chosen title, which is a nice way to make a good first impression. I'm amazed when people submit a contest entry with a poor title, or even no title at all. What a missed opportunity. The title does not have to be unique (titles can't be copyrighted) but avoid using a well-known title unless you are giving it your own spin ("Fifty Shades of Fay"). Also avoid overused or generic titles like "Hope," "Letting Go," or "The Beach."

In rare situations, you may think of a fantastic title before you even start writing. A clever or intriguing phrase may pop into your head, along with the premise for a story, but if that isn't the case, wait until you are finished writing to choose the title. If you create a title and then try to write toward it, you may unintentionally constrain yourself.

Spending time worrying about the title can delay your getting the story down and is unlikely to yield a satisfying result. Sure, you can (and probably should) come up with a working title, just to have a way of referring to the project. This can be generic and literal ("The Boy Who Couldn't Find His Way Home") to make it easy for you to distinguish it from other projects you may be working on. When the work is complete, go through the story carefully and see what comes to you.

Like the frame of a painting, the title should be designed to set the work off to its best advantage, not just package it. Ben Nyberg points out that the title is "the one point in your story where you speak *as author* directly to readers rather than through your character." He compares voicing the title to stepping in front of the curtain before the play starts to make an announcement.

The title should set the tone for the story and be compatible with the style, imagery, and tone of the story. Don't say too much and be economical with your words. *Jaws* was originally titled *The Jaws of Death.* Shortening the title actually strengthened it. Don't be too clever. *The Great Gatsby* was almost titled *Trimalchio in West Egg*, an obscure reference to first-century Roman fiction. Don't give away too much. *Gone with the Wind* was almost titled *Tomorrow Is Another Day*, which would have significantly reduced the impact of that wonderful line.

Ten Ways to Create a Title

1. Use a line of dialogue.

This works well if you have a distinctive character, setting, or genre. A line of dialogue can convey something about the story and its setting as well as the character.

2. Create an element of mystery.

Is there an obscure term, phrase, object, or activity in your story? Readers probably won't know what the title means initially, but will have an "aha" moment when they come upon the title within the story. For example, the title for the story "The Cat's Whisker" in *The Beach House* refers to a thin wire on a shortwave radio, an interesting term that provided an intriguing title.

3. Borrow interest.

Play off a well-known event or make a cultural reference. Look to popular expressions and proverbs. This can be particularly effective if you are using the term in a fresh context (Janet Evanovich's *One for the Money*).

4. Steal interest.

Well, not *steal*, exactly. Fair use allows you to take a line or phrase from a poem or a book. Common sources writers have used include the bible, Shakespeare, and poetry from writers such as William Blake, T. S. Eliot, and William Butler Yeats.

5. Incorporate action.

A title can include a possessive (*Portnoy's Complaint*), describe an activity (*Waiting to Exhale*), or indicate an earlier action (*The Spy Who Came in from the Cold*).

6. Pair unrelated words.

Think names of rock bands. You can create tension, humor, or mystery by juxtaposing words that seemingly have nothing to do with each other (*A Clockwork Orange*). Ideally, there should still be some connection to the content, even if it's just the feeling or impression the title evokes.

7. Have a little fun.

If it is a light or upbeat story, consider puns, plays on words, joke punchlines, and other sources of humor for the title. Light mysteries seem to lend themselves well to this treatment (*Cooking Can Be Murder*).

8. Go short or long.

Titles that are unusually short (*1984*) or long (*Good Omens: The Nice and Accurate Prophecies of Agnes Nutter, Witch*) stand out.

9. Don't be too literal.

Convey the content, style, or theme of the story, but don't be too obvious. You might reference something connected to the story (*Catch-22*) or make a play on words (*Time to Kill*). It might be an action your character takes, something taken out of context, or an ironic twist (*The Talented Mr. Ripley*).

10. Don't mislead the reader.

Unless the irony is clear, don't give a humorous title to a sad story or a romantic title to a story without romance. A title that deceives the reader—unless done for obvious effect—will lead to a disappointed reader.

Title Checklist

- ❒ Have you chosen a title that will make your story stand out?
- ❒ Does the title provide intrigue without giving away too much?
- ❒ Have you avoided being too literal?
- ❒ Does the title fit the genre of the story?
- ❒ Is the title distinctive and memorable?

Editing

The Editing Process

> You know you're writing well when you're throwing good stuff into the wastebasket.
>
> –Ernest Hemingway

Before getting into the specifics, a word of warning: don't start editing too soon. You will waste time if you start extensive editing before you finish writing the story. Most writers can't resist polishing a little as they go, but don't spend hours perfecting every sentence and getting each scene just right. Later you may decide on a change in the point of view or structure of the story that requires rewriting or deleting the section you spent so much time perfecting.

Editing as you go can also crush creativity. If you are critical of every sentence and examine every paragraph as you write it, you will lose your momentum, become discouraged, and possibly get off track. Hours later you may have some nice writing but no story. The same goes for fact-checking. Just flag any areas of concern for now, using highlighting or some other method that will remind you to check that section later. Writing taps the unconscious, and many writers find that things appear on the page they didn't expect. If you focus too much on the mechanics of writing, you may stand in the way of the magic.

The editing process will vary, depending upon whether you are working with a professional editor provided by the publisher, working with a professional editor you have hired yourself, or editing entirely on your own. There are many books devoted to the topic of editing, as well as many excellent references such as *The Chicago Manual of Style* (University of Chicago), *A Writer's Reference*

(Diana Hacker), and *The Copyeditor's Handbook* (Amy Einsohn), so this section is intended only as a brief overview.

If you come away with one message, let it be this: There is no substitute for professional editing. Let me say that again: There is no substitute for professional editing. Few writers have the skills to produce a well-edited book, and even those who do should not edit their own work. It is amazing how easy it is to read what you think you wrote and not what you actually wrote. Why waste all your hard work by ending up with a manuscript that contains errors?

There are three main types of editing, and you should make sure that the editor you hire has sufficient skill and extensive experience with the type of editing you are seeking. Most editors specialize in a particular type of editing, and some have an additional specialty such as technical editing, developmental editing for novels, or copyediting for newspapers.

Developmental editing is editing for basic structure, logic, character development, and other large-scale issues. This is the realm of professional developmental editors and "book doctors." Many beginning writers turn to experienced writers, local writing organizations or critique groups, conference critique sessions, or people they know who are critical readers to perform this task. Depending on the expertise of the person you choose, this can be valuable input, but that does not mean the manuscript is ready for submission or publication.

Copyediting is a line-by-line edit for grammar, punctuation, spelling, and other issues relating to the mechanics of the writing. It is a specialized skill that few nonprofessionals can duplicate. It requires not only an exceptionally keen eye and an attention to detail that borders on the pathological, but also a comprehensive knowledge of grammar, punctuation, and style conventions (which numbers are spelled out, for example). Copyeditors work to a particular style guide (*The Chicago Manual of Style* and the *Associated Press Style Guide* are two popular ones) to make sure your writing is clear, correct, and consistent.

Proofreading is a skill that seems like something anyone can do but is astonishingly difficult to do well. Professional proofreaders can find errors that escaped dozens of critical readers, editing passes, and self-reviews. They also check for often-overlooked errors such as a page number out of sequence, inconsistent character name, incorrect typeface or size, and improper paragraph indent. Proofreading is generally performed after the story is put into the design format (what used to be called typesetting).

If your short story will be published by a commercial company, the publisher will provide the editing services at no charge (unless it's a vanity or subsidy publisher), and your job will be to work with the editor to review the corrections, revise or rewrite where necessary, and check any questioned facts or references.

The publisher may or may not provide a developmental editor (more likely, a manuscript that needs developmental editing will just be rejected), but will certainly provide a copyeditor and proofreader (sometimes the same person serves in both roles). This does not absolve you of the responsibility to make sure your manuscript is error-free. It is your name, not the editor's, that will be attached to your story.

If you are planning to hire an editor yourself, you should first make sure you hire the right kind of editor. For example, don't expect developmental editors to correct grammar and punctuation. Likewise, a copyeditor will not tell you that the first six paragraphs of your story should be moved later in the story or that a scene falls flat because there is not enough action.

Self-Editing

> He who represents himself has a fool for a client.
>
> –attributed to Abraham Lincoln, but probably from an earlier source

You have wisely chosen to use a professional editor, but before sending your manuscript out, you will want to perform a self-edit to get the story in as final a form as possible. This will give you a manuscript worthy of critique readers and will likely save you money on the edit (many editors charge by the hour).

When you are revising your own work, there are several ways to approach it. All of them require an undisturbed, undistracted focus. Editing necessitates an intense attention to detail and a commitment to perfection. Flip off the television or music, silence the cell phone, turn off Facebook and email notifications, and ask family members and friends not to disturb you. Editing is the brain surgery of writing. A moment's inattention and you may cut the wrong tissue or miss a malignant error.

Your story *does* need editing. Don't kid yourself. Most writers overwrite. Cut. Cut. Cut. Cut until cutting any more will make the story worse, not better. Few manuscripts can't be improved by tightening them. It's the difference between an off-the-rack suit that fits pretty well and a custom-fit suit that has been nipped and tucked to perfection. It's natural to want to keep bits of poetic writing you're proud of, characters you like, and all those colorful details you spent so much time researching, but unless they advance the story, leave them out. Keep it lean—every word should work; every sentence should be vital.

Don't give a manuscript to your spouse, child, best friend, or neighbor and expect to get a real critique. Members of writers' clubs and critique groups generally give better feedback, but even then you are often getting input from relatively inexperienced writers like yourself. Shannon Reed wrote a clever piece for BuzzFeed titled "If Jane Austen Got Feedback From Some Guy In A Writing Workshop." Among other advice the fellow offered Jane was this helpful suggestion on her manuscript for *Pride and Prejudice*: "Why five sisters? How about just two? Combine Jane and Kitty."

If you can get an editor, librarian, or writing instructor to give you feedback, that can be useful. Beta readers (test readers similar to your target audience) can also provide useful input, especially if prompted by questions such as these: "Did _____ surprise you?" or "When did you realize that ___?" Ask specific questions about the title, the ending, the characters, key plot points, and the point of view ("Do you think the story would be more interesting if I told it from __'s point of view?" Find out what emotions the readers felt and if there were points in the story where they lost interest.

Try to be open-minded when you receive feedback. It can be difficult to listen to criticism, but even if you think the reviewers are 100 percent wrong, hear them out. Listen. They are doing you a favor by being critical. "Looks good" isn't helpful. Ask for specifics. If readers don't like a certain character, ask why. If they didn't like the ending, ask if it was too short, too long, unsatisfying, or implausible.

You may get conflicting opinions, so ask more than one person and look for consistencies or for issues you see yourself once they are pointed out. Don't make changes every time someone suggests one. Wait until you have gotten sufficient feedback to feel confident about what you need to revise and how.

Some people advocate for editing on a hard copy of the manuscript. They believe a printed document is easier to read and mark up and is a more effective way to spot errors. Others would rather edit on-screen. Word-processing software points out obvious spelling and grammatical errors; you can use the "find" function to search for common problems; and you can quickly look up definitions and synonyms online. Mistakes can be corrected immediately, and no paper is wasted.

I recommend what I call the Oreo approach: edit on-screen, then print out a copy and edit that (making the changes to your electronic document when you are finished), and then go through and edit on-screen again. Oh, and then treat yourself to some Oreos. I can almost guarantee you will find new errors each time (errors you missed during earlier passes) and you will have an excuse to eat Oreos. But not those puny mini ones or the golden ones or—God forbid—the mint or berry ones. Oreos.

As you edit, it is wise to save versions of the document under different titles (adding the current date to the file name is an easy way to keep track). When using computers, you may be tempted to just keep editing the same file, but what do you do if you deleted a scene three weeks ago and later decide to put it back in? If you have saved earlier versions, it's an easy cut-and-paste.

There are a few editing tricks that may help you drastically improve your story. Start by letting the story sit for a few days and then look at it cold, as if you were reading it for the first time. This will give you a sense of the big picture: whether the story works, the characters are engaging, the plot is plausible, and so forth. You may also pick up some obvious grammar or spelling errors, but try to focus on the story as a whole. Mark areas that seem to drag and those that seem rushed or confusing. Flag dialogue that doesn't sound authentic. Highlight sections that should be moved or that seem redundant.

Print your story and cut it into scenes. This will allow you to move them around to check structure and test whether you can eliminate (or move) the opening scene later in the story or take an exciting scene from later in the story and move it up to the front. Shifting the arrangement of scenes can increase the drama. Just make sure you don't lose the reader in the process. Look for paragraphs or scenes that don't seem to add anything. Cut them out and put them aside. When you are finished, read the edited version and make sure there are no holes in the story. If you decide to change your mind, it will be easy to retrieve the section you cut.

Another technique is to retype the story. Short stories are easy enough to retype from a printed copy, and, in doing so, you will often find errors or make improvements.

One of my favorite tricks is something I call "Off with their heads!" (I'm an *Alice in Wonderland* fan). When you think you are finished with a story or essay, try deleting or moving the first paragraph, first few paragraphs, or even the first scene so that the piece starts *in media res* (in the midst of things). Opening in the middle of the action hooks the reader and gets the story off to a fast start.

Read the manuscript out loud. This can help identify awkward sentences, unrealistic dialogue, poor sentence rhythm, distracting words or phrases, bad pacing, dull patches, and too much explanation.

Take the time to do a careful self-edit. Don't rely on your word-processing software to catch errors. Machines make mistakes too.

Developmental Editing

> It was like removing layers of crumpled brown paper from an awkwardly shaped parcel, and revealing the attractive present which it contained.
>
> –Diana Athill, *Stet: An Editor's Life*

Developmental editing, sometimes called "editing for structure" or the "content edit," is big-picture stuff, and that's why it has to come first. Sure, if you happen to notice a faulty fact or a mangled modifier, there's no reason you can't correct it on the fly, but don't get bogged down polishing the leaves on a tree when that entire forest may end up as sawdust.

Very few writers underwrite. These folks usually end up as advertising copywriters crafting text for billboards, but some are fiction writers who have realized that when they underwrite a novel, they end up with the beginnings of a winning short story. Cutting for length nearly always improves a story. Like a skilled butcher, cut the fat from your story until you end up with a tasty little nugget. Strategic cutting creates a story that has more dramatic impact, is more enjoyable to read, and has more punch.

Start by making sure you haven't started the story too early. Eliminate any "throat clearing" and unnecessary background—get right to the action. Watch the transitions too. Cut scenes of characters traveling from one place to another (unless something else is going on).

If the story is too long in your own or an editor's opinion, look for flabby writing. Tighten sentences, look for verbose dialogue, and eliminate paragraphs or scenes that don't advance the story. Stephen King says that one of the best pieces of advice he ever got was a scribbled comment from an editor he had submitted a story to. It read: "Not bad, but PUFFY. You need to revise for length. Formula: 2nd Draft = 1st Draft –10%, Good luck." If the story is too long for a publication's guidelines or a contest submission and you've already written a nice, tight story, look at cutting scenes rather than crimping your writing. If the story loses power, find another outlet for it rather than ruin the story to meet a word count.

If the story is too short, consider adding another character, showing some scenes that occurred "offstage," or expanding the viewpoint character's motivation rather than just padding the writing with excess, unnecessary verbiage. If the results don't please you, look for outlets for short-shorts (flash fiction or microfiction). This is a growing market, and perhaps you have a knack for it.

Editing for point of view is essential and should be done carefully. Make sure the point of view you've chosen and the character whose head you are in is the right one for telling the story. Watch for any slips in who is reporting the action, and whose thoughts the reader is privy to. Be particularly careful if you changed the point of view. Look for any places where the person telling the story wouldn't know about a key event or wasn't present for an important piece of dialogue. Make sure your point of view is consistent.

Look for logic and timing inconsistencies. If the story begins in summer and four months pass, the weather should have gotten considerably colder unless you are in an area where the temperature doesn't change. If many years pass, your character's behavior, habits, and, to some extent, speech should change, but your character (unless it's explained) should remain consistent (in general appearance, temperament, personality, and background).

Check your characters. If you are running long, look to see if you can combine the "work" of two characters (the purpose they serve in the story) into one character. Are your main characters fully developed? Is there some complexity to their characters (they're not stereotypes) and some individuality (they're not all you)? Is there sufficient conflict (characters with competing goals)?

Watch for scene-stealers. It's okay to have vibrant, attention-getting secondary characters but don't let them steal the spotlight from the viewpoint character. Make sure that the primary character is the focal point for the story and that the reader is more emotionally engaged with that character than the subsidiary characters.

Have you wandered off topic? Even an exceptional piece of writing, if it doesn't contribute to moving the story along, should be cut and perhaps used elsewhere. You may even find that your digression is another story. Check between-the-scenes material. Make sure you don't have excess baggage slowing down your story. It's particularly important to take out lengthy explanations and accounts of actions that took place elsewhere.

Check for explanations that don't need to be there. My husband gives directions like it's a sightseeing tour: "Go three blocks until you see a large oak tree on the left next to a house with blue shutters. Keep going until you get to a stop sign. There will be a gas station on one corner and a café on the other. Continue another six blocks..." You get the idea. We don't need to know about trees, gas stations, cafés, and stop signs unless they are pertinent. Check your narration for unnecessary information (unless you are intentionally providing red herrings).

Make sure your mood is consistent and you haven't thrown cold water on an emotional moment. The mood in your story can change as your character confronts and resolves the conflict, but don't shock readers by sudden shifts (unless it's for effect). If your story is a light romance and the love interest is suddenly found murdered, readers will not be happy about it. Check for unevenness in tone, pacing, or style. Avoid sections that start out as one thing and then shift gears, jarring the reader.

Are you relying on large blocks of narrative to tell your story, rather than "acting it out" in scenes? This is a sign that your plot may be too complex for the length of the story. Stories written this way sound like a synopsis: "First she said goodbye to the kids, then she drove to a meeting, and the next day she had lunch with Joe, and a week later she..." If you find yourself struggling with the problem of overly complicated plots again and again, you are probably better suited for writing novels.

Stories that are too slight often garner a "meh" from judges and readers. These are stories in which the conflict is not big or important enough, the character isn't engaging enough, or there just isn't enough at stake to make people care. Look for a way to incorporate another idea, conflict, character, or twist. Maybe you can tap into a deeper theme. If you are unable to do that, you may need to shelve the idea and come up with a different plot. All is not lost. You may be able to repurpose characters, scenes, snippets of dialogue, setting, or other elements in another story. In writing, nothing is wasted!

When you think you're finished, here are some additional things to try:

1. Add something to the end of the story that connects back to the beginning.

2. See if there are some pieces of information you can keep from the reader to create surprise at the end.

3. Look for places to add humor (a funny word, awkward situation, character quirk).

Copyediting

> **You might be strutting around unaware your zipper is open, proud as ever of your manuscript—not realizing others are "speechless" for the wrong reasons.**
>
> –Ashlyn Forge, *Self-Editing on a Penny*

Copyediting is sometimes called "line editing" and for good reason. This is where you look at your story line by line, checking every sentence, every word, and every punctuation mark. Even if your story will go through a professional editor, do your best to make sure you are saying what you mean to say.

Copyediting normally comes after developmental editing because you don't want to waste time going line by line through sections that may get deleted, but you should spend some time copyediting the manuscript yourself before sending it to anyone else to read. If you are at a point where you want feedback on your story, take the time to polish it up a bit so readers aren't so distracted by small errors that they miss larger issues. Grammar and spelling errors also send a message of unprofessionalism, and no matter who is reading your story, you do not want to give that impression.

Check for common errors (discussed in a following section), especially those that spellcheckers may miss, such as "to" instead of "too" and "your" instead of "you're." Look for words ending in "ly" to root out adverbs and words ending in "ing" (often gerunds or dangling participles). Those sentences can often be rewritten using stronger verbs and nouns. Minimize adverbs and adjectives by choosing verbs and nouns carefully (Instead of "He quickly pushed the long, thin, pointed metal stick into the large cube of marinated lamb," write "He skewered the kebob."). This tightens the writing and makes it more interesting. Maintain an active voice ("She socked him in the face.") rather than passive voice ("His face was hit by her fist.").

Don't beat around the bush. Instead of "at this moment in time," write "now." And while you are at it, get rid of clichés like "don't beat around the bush." Remember: "Any fool can make things bigger, more complex. It takes a touch of genius—and a lot of courage—to move in the opposite direction" (Albert Einstein).

Check for too many words of three syllables or more and for overblown words and phrases. Adding complication won't make your writing seem more important and may even make you look silly. My husband once fainted and later noticed that the insurance form referred to the event as "loss of posture." Unless you are writing an academic book (and perhaps even then), don't force readers to use a machete to hack through your prose.

Be aware of your writing tics. Every writer has them. A word you use too much, a phrase you tend to repeat, or a punctuation mark—like a dash, for example—that pops up—like crabgrass—throughout your story. Most writers have a few favorite words that they use too frequently (an editor who reviewed this manuscript pointed out that I used "a lot" a lot). I deleted a lot of them.

You may give more than one character a particular manner of speech (starting sentences with "Well," for example). If one character does it, it's the character's habit, but if more than one does it, it's *your* habit. These tics may be difficult for you to notice, but readers will find them annoying. This is where an honest critique can really help.

Look for opportunities to make your words pop. Where appropriate, use devices such as alliteration, metaphor, and rhyming words to give the story a lyrical quality. Look for rhythm in your writing. Like poetry, carefully written prose can be beautiful. You have to choose words anyway—why not choose the ones that will make the passage a delight to read?

This is also the time to look at the structure of paragraphs and sentences. Do your sentences vary in length and style? Unless you want your story to be a sleep aid, have some short snappy sentences and some longer, more complex sentences. Make sure you don't have giant blocks of unrelenting text or, at the other end of the spectrum, page after page of short dialogue exchanges that will read like a ping-pong game.

Grammar checkers (and spellcheckers, for that matter) don't catch everything and are sometimes wrong. They will flag sentences with unusual structure such as sentences that are normally phrased as a question but are being used as a statement, incomplete or run-on sentences used for effect (yes, that is permissible), foreign spellings of words used intentionally, and other unconventional language.

Eliminate clichés; they are the sign of a lazy writer. Come up with a new expression, turn a cliché sideways, or just describe the situation. Clichés can be stock phrases like "thick as pea soup," or they can be descriptions that have been overdone ("she tossed her raven tresses"). Character traits and situations can be cliché as well. The burly handyman, the smart kid with thick glasses, the character with amnesia—these are familiar clichés that have no place in your story. Also watch for your own pet phrases. Expressions like "at the end of the day" are annoying enough the first time around. We don't need to hear them twice.

Eliminate, remove, and get rid of redundancies (see what I did there?). These can take many forms. The most obvious is a repeated word. These can be typos like like this, or they can be poor word choice like this: "He looked up. She looked fantastic, as usual." Make sure you haven't said the same thing twice, with different wording. A common error is overlapping adjectives (adjectives you may have piled on to add emphasis but that don't add anything). For example, "dark, swarthy skin" is redundant because "swarthy" also means "dark." Adding even one adjective to some nouns can create a redundancy, as in these examples: "honest truth," "free gift," and "join together."

Some words are absolutes and cannot be qualified without redundancy. For example, the word "unique" does not just mean "unusual." Something is either unique (one of a kind) or isn't. It can't be "really unique," "very unique," or a "unique one of a kind." Here are some additional examples of redundancy:

7 p.m. in the evening

It was snowing. White flakes fell from the sky.

It was blue in color.

She blinked her eyes.

He stood up.

Examine the story for other forms of repetition. Don't have characters explain what they've learned if the reader was present when they learned it. Don't repeatedly remind the reader that a character is messy or that the house she lives in is a white colonial. Make sure that you don't have two different characters driving the same type of car, reading the same book, or wearing the same watch (unless it's intentional). And don't have the character mention the same habit over and over. (We get it—he drinks Chivas.)

Give your manuscript a critical line-by-line edit so that it's (as Mary Poppins would say) practically perfect in every way before sending it to readers for input or to a professional editor. By putting in a little extra effort now, you will save time and money later and reduce the chance that your final story will contain errors.

Proofreading

> There are Two Typos of People in This World: Those Who Can Edit And Those Who Can't
>
> –title of a book by Jarod Kintz

Proofreaders are nitpickers, and that's a good thing. Errors in grammar, spelling, and punctuation pull the reader out of the fictional world and brand the author as an amateur. Mistakes can sneak through despite many examinations by multiple readers, and it's even easier for mistakes to creep in near the end. I once received a story submission that had at the bottom: "Copywrite 2015."

Read every word. Examine every little thing. *Every* little thing. It is surprisingly easy to leave a word without meaning to. Did you spot it? Reread the sentence carefully. Our minds often fill in words that fit our expectations. Expect to see, "It is surprisingly easy to leave a word out without meaning to" and that's what you may see, whether or not the word "out" is actually there. Reading each word individually will also help you pick up errors such as "car" instead of "cat" or "hare" instead of "hard." Look for errors of the mind (where you wrote "stake" but meant "steak" or even "state"), formatting errors (an extra space or line, for example), and inconsistencies.

Don't feel that you can make mistakes just to be artistic. Learn grammar as part of perfecting your craft. You have to know the rules to break the rules.

If you've skipped lightly over this section thinking that your exceptional premise, captivating theme, and mesmerizing writing will win the hearts of editors (who will then overlook those inconsequential grammatical errors, misspellings, and typos), consider this comment, from Weldon Burge, executive editor and founder of Smart Rhino Publications, who evaluates and selects short stories for anthologies: "As an editor, the number one problem I see is a lack of editing and proofreading in the stories submitted. It may not seem fair to many writers, but I will stop reading a story if it is littered with misspellings and grammatical errors, which are often on the first page. I may continue to read if the story is compelling enough and I think I can work with the writer to refine the story, but I'm far more likely to accept stories that don't require more work on my part."

Common Errors

1. **Double spaces**

   It is no longer correct to put two spaces between sentences; there should only be one space after the period.

2. **Shifting tense**

   Make sure you are not shifting tense within a scene. If you shift tense to indicate flashbacks or memories, be consistent so you don't confuse readers.

3. **Changing point of view**

   If you switch the point of view from one character to another character, or change from first or second person to third person, be consistent. If you are telling a story from one character's point of view, be careful to stay inside that character's head and not suddenly describe the thoughts, feelings, or unseen actions of another character (except through a narrator).

4. **Age-inappropriate characters**

   If you write about children or teens, make sure their dialogue and actions ring true. No matter what the age of your character, the thoughts and actions should be plausible for that age. Also make sure the character names are believable. Check lists of baby names by year to choose names appropriate for the characters' ages.

5. **Time-inappropriate characters**

   If you set your story in another time period (even just a few years from the present day), make sure that the characters' names, appearances, actions, and behavior are appropriate. Confirm any location and event details.

6. Spelling errors

Check for words that can be spelled more than one way. "It's" means "it is." Do not include an apostrophe unless you mean "it is." Other frequently confused words are your/you're, their/there/they're, then/than, and peak/peek/pique. Confirm spellings of businesses, streets, towns, and products (especially trade names), as these may not be standard words. Make sure you have spelled character names and places consistently.

7. Punctuation and writing tics

Many people have a punctuation mark they tend to overuse. The most commonly overused marks are the dash and the exclamation mark. Go back through your manuscript and look for places where a comma might replace the dash and substitute periods for exclamation points. If you tend to overuse certain words or expressions, check for these as well.

8. Excessive use of italics

Italic text is distracting. Italics can be used for emphasis, unspoken thoughts, and foreign words, but take care not to overuse it. If you have a long quotation (a letter, for example), it is better to indent than to use italics.

9. Incorrect dialogue tags

Dialogue tags must be actions that result in speech. Tags that indicate any other actions are incorrect. Tags should be unobtrusive ("he said") or absent (when it's clear who is speaking). Avoid distracting tags ("he bellowed explosively").

10. Omitted words

When you are extremely familiar with a piece of writing, it is easy to read it the way you think it is written, rather than the way it is actually written. Missed words are therefore easily overlooked. Some ways to check for this include reading the work aloud, having others read it, and setting it aside and then reading it again when it is not as fresh in your mind.

11. Adjectives and adverbs instead of strong nouns and verbs

Adjectives are words that describe a noun. Some are necessary, but many can be eliminated by choosing a stronger noun. Instead of writing "big house," use "mansion." Adverbs perform a similar function for verbs and are also often unnecessary. Instead of writing "he walked slowly," write "he strolled." And avoid useless modifiers such as "very," "really," and "quite."

12. Trite phrases and clichés

Phrases like "black as night," "bulging biceps," and "like mother's milk" are a sign of a lazy writer. Look for fresh or unexpected comparisons and descriptions rather than falling back on the familiar and overused.

13. Filter words

Using words like "saw," "felt," and "heard," instead of conveying the sensation directly separates the reader from the action. Instead of writing, "She saw the car coming toward her," write "The car came toward her."

14. Use of "it" without a clear reference

Do a search/find for "it" and, where possible, replace "it" with a word that clarifies what you are referring to. Never use "it" unless it is obvious what the "it" is.

Editing Checklist

❐ Have you considered hiring a professional editor?

❐ Do you understand how developmental editing, copyediting, and proofreading differ?

❐ Have you eliminated scenes or blocks of dialogue that do not advance the story?

❐ Has the point of view stayed consistent throughout the story (unless it's intentional and you have indicated a break)?

❐ Have you eliminated redundant words, phrases, and sentences?

❐ Have you checked for overused words and phrases and any personal writing tics?

❐ Do your sentences vary in length and style?

❐ Have you deleted any trite phrases and clichés?

❐ Have you checked your manuscript for common errors?

Facts, Logic, and Lawyers

Fact-Checking

> If a writer of prose knows enough about what he is writing about, he may omit things that he knows and the reader, if the writer is writing truly enough, will have a feeling of those things as strongly as though the writer had stated them. The dignity of movement of an iceberg is due to only one-eighth of it being above water.
>
> –Ernest Hemingway, *Death in the Afternoon*

Research and fact-checking is essential for fiction as well as nonfiction. Research your location, time period, and other details extensively. Study the climate, landscape, styles of homes, and traffic conditions for any locations you reference in your story. Use the correct terminology for medical, technical, or specialty occupations or processes described in your story. You won't want to use all the research, but you will write more confidently as a result of knowing the information. Errors pull readers out of the story and raise questions about the veracity of your writing.

Check everything. Verify every date, address, name, specialized term, foreign phrase, historical detail, and fact. If you use a specific time and place for the story, confirm that your seasonal and weather details are accurate. Verify the spellings of street names, cities, and other details.

There's a reason people say "write what you know." It is difficult to write convincingly about a place you've never been. Make one wrong assumption, get one fact wrong, insert one detail that doesn't ring true, and you will lose your reader. Even if you are familiar with the topic or location, verify your details. Make sure your dialogue (words, spellings, slang, colloquialisms, technical terminology, accents, and style of speech) match the time period, location, and character you are writing about. Don't assume anything.

When you check facts, make sure your source is reliable. In general, government and academic (university) sources are an ideal place to start. Avoid biased sources such as political groups, organizations involved with a cause, opinion-based content, and sources that have a vested interest in a particular point of view or outcome. Be careful with Internet sources. Determine the ownership and mission of the website before assuming its content is reliable.

Many people rely on Wikipedia as a fast and easy resource, but on its own page Wikipedia includes this word of caution: "It is important to use Wikipedia carefully if it is intended to be used as a research source, since individual articles will, by their nature, vary in quality and maturity." Most universities do not accept Wikipedia as a reference; Harvard University warns students about it, saying: "There is a considerable risk in relying on this source," and follows that up with an anecdote about a student who, while writing a paper about the limitations of Wikipedia, posted a fictional entry for himself that stated he was the mayor of a small town in China. The entry remained live for years.

You can access a list of vetted fact-checking resources here: http://www.journaliststoolbox.org/archive/general-resources-fact-checkinglibraries.

Logic

> By all means let the writer of short stories reduce the technical trick to its minimum—as the cleverest actresses put on the least paint; but let him always bear in mind that the surviving minimum is the only bridge between the reader's imagination and his.
>
> –Edith Wharton

When you write a story, you are creating a world. This is easy to see in genres such as science fiction, where the story takes place in a completely created world, but even a story that takes place in current time, in your home town, with no supernatural elements, is going to take place in a world you create. For this reason, one of the writer's jobs is to maintain a natural assumption of reality, a sense of plausibility that allows the reader to step into—and stay within—the world you create. The greater the improbability of the story, the more sure the hand has to be that tells the reader "this is how things happen here." Once your readers suspend disbelief and have confidence in you, you can take them on some pretty wild rides, but make a misstep, and you will break the spell, and readers will lose their connection to your world.

The illusion can be shattered in any number of ways: an abrupt change in point of view, a logic error (How could it still be light at 7 p.m. when it's supposed to be December in Boston?), an erroneous description, grammatical or spelling errors, or writing that simply calls attention to itself.

Take a close look at your story for logic errors that involve the props in your story. These mistakes are called continuity errors in the movies, where they are sometimes easy to spot (a character has a hat on in one part of the scene, then the hat is inexplicably missing and reappears later). In writing this might take the form of a character stating that the power has been turned off in an earlier scene and later flipping on a light, or someone putting a book on a bookshelf and another character picking the book up off a table. Make sure that clothing items you mention match the season and weather for the location. If you state the type of car, find out whether it has two doors or four before you have someone getting into the back seat.

If you are writing from the point of view of someone of a different gender, culture, or religion than yours, make sure you don't have the character doing or saying something inappropriate to that background (unless it's explained). I remember a funny scene from an episode of *Law & Order: Criminal Intent* in which detectives Goren and Eames are examining a crime scene in a public bathroom. Goren, a male detective, speculated that the female victim would have entered the stall, put her pocketbook on the floor, and then sat down. Eames, the female detective, corrected him, saying the woman would have hung her pocketbook on the hook. Goren refuted this because it would have been easier to just put it on the floor, but Eames was adamant. A woman would have hung her pocketbook on a hook rather than place it on the floor of a public restroom. Goren finally concedes, saying that it must be a "girl thing." A funny moment, and one that points out a small, but telling, detail that might have seemed wrong to a female viewer.

Make sure that your stories don't sound dated. The writer's frame of reference affects many of the details within a story. If you are an older writer who is writing a story that takes place in present day, make sure to check names, prices, salaries, car models, medical terms, slang and popular expressions, and other details to make sure they are current. I once received a story that described a ten-year-old girl being delighted to receive a doll. In 1940 maybe, but today's children are more likely to receive robotic toys or electronic games.

Names seem to be a particular problem. While I was working on this section, a writer submitted a picture book featuring children named Jane, Tommy, and David. I can probably guess the writer's age within a decade. Those are not current children's names.

You also need to make sure that your timing makes sense. For example, if you are describing a character who is defusing a bomb that is set to go off in ten seconds, you can't take four or five pages to describe the wires, the sweat running down his face, and the approaching sirens. Likewise, you can't have someone who was gardening in the backyard answer the front doorbell immediately. Also verify that the sequence of events makes sense. Check especially carefully if you have moved scenes around. Do any of the characters know something they shouldn't? Do you refer to events that haven't happened yet? Have conversations taken place out of order?

Your fictional world can be anything you want: a 1950s suburban development, a village in Kenya, an outpost on another planet, New York in the year 2563. As the writer, you set the rules. Is it winter or spring (or an invented season)? Can humans breathe under water and animals breathe fire? Are apples purple and the size of grapefruit? It's all up to you.

There is only one thing you must remember: once you set the rules, you must be consistent. This also applies to the tone of the story. If you write about a dark, serious situation, you can't suddenly turn the story into a madcap adventure. Readers start with some expectations. If you mislead them, you run the risk of disappointing or even angering them. This includes the title and (in the case of a book) the cover. A story called "The Lewes Ferry, a Five-Pound Dog, and Romance" (by Nancy Powichroski Sherman) is signaling the reader that it is likely to be a light, romantic romp. The ferry shouldn't sink, the dog shouldn't die, and there should be some romance somewhere.

Legal Issues

> **All artists are protected by copyright—and we should be the first to respect copyright.**
>
> –Bill Cannon

Let's start right off with a disclaimer: I am not an attorney, and this section is not in any way intended to replace legal advice from an attorney. I am including this information because I have discovered that many beginning writers don't even think about liability issues, and you can get yourself into some real difficulty, especially if you are self-publishing and don't have a publisher's legal team looking out for you.

With written material, most legal problems boil down to content ownership issues or exposure to libel claims. Either one can cause you grief. Intellectual property, like any other kind of property, is owned by a particular person or company, so another person or company can't just take it and use it. You wouldn't just hop in a car you saw on the street and take it for a spin, would you? Even if the keys were in it? No. Because you don't have that right, even if it's just sitting there. Like a story on the Internet.

Written works, even if unpublished, are owned by the writer. Published works are owned by the copyright holder, which is usually, but not always (it depends on rights granted to the publisher by the contract the writer signed), the writer. This means that, while you own the rights to your own work, you give up those rights if you sign a contract that gives the ownership to someone else. It also means that you cannot use another person's work without permission. This includes poems, lengthy quotations from books, song lyrics, and portions of film or movie scripts. And it includes material on the Internet.

The only works like these you are free to use are those in the public domain, which usually means that the work is old enough that the copyright has expired. You can, for example, use material from James Fenimore Cooper, but James Patterson is going to cost you. Never assume that because something is on the Internet it's in the public domain.

The only exception is "fair use," which is something of a moving target but has to do with what type of material you are using, how you're using it, how much of it you're using, and whether your use deprives the copyright holder of income. Do some research before assuming your use would be considered fair. Here is a source that provides additional information: http://fairuse.stanford.edu/overview/fair-use/four-factors.

When it comes to copyright, owning a copy of the work is not the same as owning the rights to the work. For example, if you found or bought a diary or other written document, that doesn't mean you have the right to publish it or use it in a published story without permission.

Most writers base their characters, at least in part, on people they have known, but they combine attributes, change identifying details, or otherwise disguise the descriptions so the individuals are no longer recognizable. Unless you want to risk legal problems, you should be extremely cautious when using real people in your writing, even if they are friends or family members.

Public figures (note the word "public") have less expectation of privacy than the average person. Descriptions, and even photographs, of celebrities going about their lives are often published without problems. Public figures may complain, but unless the written account is known to be untrue, designed to cause harm, and damages the person's reputation, lack of privacy is the price they pay for fame. That said, celebrities have reputations to protect and lots of money for attorney fees, so if you do get sued, you can end up spending a serious amount of money defending yourself, even if the lawsuit is baseless.

We had two stories in recent Rehoboth Beach Reads books that featured public figures. One was a fictional account that originally involved Oprah Winfrey. It included several joking, but negative comments and was obviously not based on anything she had ever actually done. I asked the author to change the name and disguise the details to avoid any possibility of a lawsuit. Another story featured an author's account of seeing rock musician Dave Grohl in a restaurant. The story was true and not disparaging in any way. That story was published using the celebrity's name.

It's a different situation when you drag your neighbor, ex-husband, or mother-in-law into a story. Even if what you describe is true, people who are not public figures have a legal right to privacy. You should not use a real individual's name, photo, or identifying information without permission. Even if the depiction is positive, you can get into trouble for using someone's likeness, name, or identifying information for commercial purposes. This is true even if that person is dead. Here is an overview of how to use real people in your writing: http://helensedwick.com/how-to-use-real-people-in-your-writing.

Facts, Logic, and Lawyers Checklist

- ❒ Have you verified all of your facts?
- ❒ Have you checked and rechecked dates, names, spellings, figures, and other details?
- ❒ Are your names, dialogue, setting, and details true to the time period (even if the time is current)?
- ❒ Is the world portrayed in your story logical?
- ❒ Does the time line of the story make sense?
- ❒ If you've used copyrighted material, is it fair use?
- ❒ If your use of copyrighted material goes beyond fair use, did you obtain written permission or determine that it was in the public domain?
- ❒ Have you been careful when referring to public figures in your story?
- ❒ If you used real people in your story, have you disguised them well?

Marketing Short Stories

Identifying Markets

> I find that most people don't know what a story is until they sit down to write one. Then they find themselves writing a sketch with an essay woven through it, or an essay with a sketch woven through it, or an editorial with a character in it, or a case history with a moral, or some other mongrel thing.
>
> –Flannery O'Connor, "The Nature and Aim of Fiction," *Mystery and Manners*

The "build it and they will come" approach works in movies, but seldom in real life. "Discoverability" is key—how will readers find your work? Today's writers are urged to build a "platform," become masters of social media, develop a fan base, and mold a personal brand. For now, let's just talk about how to get a short story into a place where people will find it and read it.

Unless you write only for yourself, think about where and how you'd like to publish your story before you even begin writing. There are large markets for some stories and smaller markets for others, so do some research and check out the outlets that are available.

Magazines and other publications target niches. A niche is a small space or cubbyhole. It doesn't sound appealing, but it can provide a path to publication, especially for beginning writers. In marketing, a niche is a specialized group of customers. Think how much easier it would be to market a product to female dog owners between the ages of sixty and eighty who live in Chicago, Illinois, than to market to everyone. You can skip national advertising and focus on Chicago-area newspapers (targeting the geography and age—older people tend to read newspapers), women's magazines (targeting the gender), and posters in pet shops (targeting the interest). Even publications that seem untargeted (literary journals, for example) are targeting a niche (sophisticated readers who enjoy high-level writing).

Think about what you want to write. What do you care deeply about? What kinds of stories do you like to read? What makes you angry? What do you love? Was there an experience you had that connects to one of these? How can you transfer that experience to a character in a story? Knowing this information may help you target your story.

Know your audience. If you are writing for a magazine, research the subscriber base to determine their interests and preferences. If you are writing for a contest, read the stories that won in previous years. It's not that you are writing to a recipe, but by understanding your potential readers, and learning more about what the people who are choosing the works like, you will be more likely to see your story in print.

One of the wonderful things about short stories is that they can often be sold more than once. Check guidelines carefully, but many magazines and especially anthologies will accept stories that were first published elsewhere, providing the author has the rights to it (see the discussion of contest red flags in the section on Contests and Awards).

For writers wanting to publish, one of the most difficult challenges is getting the attention of an agent or publisher. How does one stand out from the thousands of competing manuscripts? Well, one way is to find a niche. A niche is as appealing to publishers as it is to any other marketing entity. And now, more than ever, marketing is key to getting published. Even if you plan to self-publish—in fact, especially if you do—marketing is an essential consideration. You can write a general fiction book, but unless you target a niche, you will find it extremely difficult to get noticed by the world at large.

A variety of different kinds of niches like these are available to writers:

- Geographic (city, state, region)
- Interest group (pet owners, veterans, parents of disabled children)
- Genre (mystery, steampunk, historical romance)
- Reader age (toddler, young adult, senior)
- Style/format of writing (novella, short story, flash fiction)

Ideally, the niche you choose connects with an area of expertise or strong interest, or at the very least a topic you are willing to research extensively. An attractive niche is one that has an identifiable audience and a way of reaching that audience. Do some research within your area of expertise or interest and find out what's already been done. An ideal combination is a topic that has been covered a little (so you know there is interest) but has not been overdone.

Writing to a niche means consciously considering marketing, but not destroying your writing for the sake of marketing. You can take the story you planned to write and set it in a specific place (geographic targeting) or incorporate an issue or theme with specialized appeal. This does not mean that you write a Western and then set it in Orlando, Florida (unless you're going for humor), or that you turn a wonderful story about friendship into a lecture about animal rights, but look for ways to match your story to a specific audience. In fact, you may already have a niche audience for a story you've written.

A niche can help you identify outlets for your story. For example, a story geared toward older women might be marketed to senior-oriented magazines. If the story were historical fiction, it might be sold to a historical society magazine or be submitted to a historical fiction anthology.

Many magazines and anthologies have a theme (often one that targets a niche). For example, *Delaware Beach Life* is a regional publication (geographic niche) that publishes short stories that have a regional connection. Target that niche with a story about a Delaware ship captain and you have a chance of having your story selected. Submit a story about dogsledding in Alaska, and your chances are zero, no matter how terrific the story.

Theme is another way to target a niche. If you plan to self-publish a collection of your own short stories, you may want to consider organizing the stories around an appealing theme or popular genre. Readers like stories that have a connection, whether that connection is a character, setting, style, or subject matter. Targeting a niche gives you a thread to tie the stories together *and* a marketing advantage.

You should be conscious of whether there is a market for your story (if publishing it is your goal), but never write to today's trend. "The last thing you want is an author saying, 'That's what's selling right now, so that's what I'm going to write,'" says Julie Strauss-Gabel, publisher of Dutton Children's Books. "That's the point at which a trend gets icky."

Magazines

> A good many young writers make the mistake of enclosing a stamped, self-addressed envelope big enough for the manuscript to come back in. This is too much of a temptation to the editor.
>
> –Ring Lardner, *How to Write Short Stories (With Samples)*

Magazines can be ideal places for submitting short stories, providing they publish the sort of story you write and they accept submissions from freelance writers. To identify potential outlets for your work, consult the *Writer's Market*, an annual publication put out by Writer's Digest Books. You can buy it, purchase the online version, or use it at your public library. It lists magazines by genre and includes basic information on what they publish, how to submit, and whom to contact. New Pages (www.newpages.com) and Poets & Writers (www.pw.org) are other useful resources.

Pay particular attention to magazines that have themed issues, where the stories submitted must match the theme. Create a database of the magazines you most want to submit to, along with the acceptable lengths, genres, submission windows, and other key factors such as theme issues. Keep in mind that print magazines have long lead times. If you want to submit a holiday story, you will need to send it long before that time of year (guidelines usually provide the publication's deadlines).

One advantage of using the library for research is that the library may also have copies of some of the magazines you are considering, thus giving you a chance to see what material they've published in the past, which is an excellent indication of what they might publish in the future. In fact, as a standard practice look at a minimum of three issues of a magazine before submitting.

Read stories the magazine has published and look for patterns beyond their stated genre. Do the stories tend to feature younger (or older) characters? Is there a pattern to the settings (mainly urban vs. mainly rural, for example)? Is one point of view predominant? Is the main character typically a woman or a man? Is it a literary journal or an entertainment magazine? If it's a genre magazine (science fiction or fantasy, for example), do the stories tend to be a specific kind (futuristic Earth scenarios) or stick to a particular tradition (mythological foundations)? Find a good fit for your story or tweak it to make it a better fit.

Magazines that accept outside submissions all have guidelines for writers. If you don't see them on the website, contact the publication and request them. Then read the guidelines carefully. Magazines generally state what genres, lengths, and types of stories they use and offer insights to their criteria for selection. Consider the guidelines firm. Guidelines are the editor saying, "Here's how to make me say 'yes.'" They sometimes even provide helpful information such as the best ways for new writers to break in or topics they're particularly interested in.

If a magazine buys three 2,000-word stories a month but only one 5,000-word story, consider writing a shorter story or adapting your story, if you can do so without compromising it. If you are a beginner, start small. Magazines give the most ink to writers they feel confident about—well-known authors or writers they have worked with before.

Another way to identify magazines for submissions is to look on the copyright page or in the acknowledgments of an anthology you like to see where the stories have been previously published.

Literary magazines are extremely competitive (especially the top ones). One author said it was like getting into Harvard, only harder. However, publication in a literary magazine can be a big career boost and may even help you attract an agent or publisher. In fact, agents and publishers actively look through literary journals for new writers and often approach them directly after having seen their work in these publications.

Agents and editors you submit to will take you more seriously if some of your stories have already appeared in reputable journals and anthologies. Start with lower tier or local literary journals, but if you have a story you think is particularly strong, take a shot at one of the big names.

Anthologies

> Instead of you standing alone on a virtual corner with your signpost, hoping people will notice you, participating in an anthology means you now have ten other authors standing on other virtual street corners and holding their own signposts, all pointing in the same direction.
>
> –Jen Blood, "5 Tips for Publishing Your Own Anthology"

You may be able to get your story included in a short story anthology, particularly if it fits a specific theme or genre. You might, for example, find a publisher putting together a group of mystery stories with a food theme. If you have or could write a story that fits the theme, then that could be a perfect opportunity.

If you want to self-publish a collection of short stories, consider using a theme, a set of characters, a setting, or some other element that links the stories. This will help with marketing the stories, because most readers will not be drawn to a collection of random short stories by an author they don't know. If you do publish your own work, you should know that it may make it less appealing to a publisher, so you should consider trying to get the story published in a journal before publishing it in your own collection.

Whether or not you plan to publish your stories as an anthology, if you have found a group of characters, a setting, an unusual premise, or a unique approach, consider a succession of stories that work as a series. They don't have to be like chapters in a book, or follow each other chronologically, but if readers respond to the first story, they may be eager for more. When you have enough stories, you can publish them as a book.

Contests and Awards

> You rarely win, but sometimes you do.
>
> –Harper Lee

Contests and awards competitions can be a relatively easy way for a beginning writer to gain publishing credentials. Contests force you to read guidelines and write to a deadline and word count, which is practice for becoming a professional writer. They also give you experience with editing, revising, and proofreading your work. Contests are generally inexpensive to enter, and if you win, you may get cash, publication, or both. They also provide a chance to have your writing evaluated objectively. Publication gives you credibility as a professional writer and adds to your bio for future projects.

Even established writers can benefit from contests. Winning a contest can get your writing noticed, give you publicity opportunities, and provide networking potential. Additional publications help you build a fan base. You maintain ownership (check the guidelines carefully to confirm) and can sell your work elsewhere, so you are not giving anything away.

There are some dubious contests out there, so it pays to do a little research. Start by determining who is running the competition. Is the company or organization running the contest or offering the award legitimate? Is it a nonprofit organization hosting a contest primarily for its members? A profit-making company looking to create a commercially viable book? A vanity (pay-for-publication) publisher seeking new clients? An organization wanting to recognize literary merit? A writing services company wanting to sell coaching, editing, or publishing services? Poke around online and ask fellow writers about their experiences.

What is the purpose of the contest or award? Be wary of awards programs that have dozens of entry categories, each accompanied by a high fee. If the reward is publication, verify that the winning stories from previous years were actually published and examine the quality of the publication. Make sure that the "contest" is not simply a way to get people to pay to submit content that the organization can post online (and make money from) without any benefit to you. Be wary of contests that promise literary agency representation (which may be the same company under another name or require the purchase of their editing services).

Evaluate the cost of entering the contest. The fee should not be more than twenty to thirty dollars, unless the contest is extremely prestigious or has an enormous cash prize. Weigh the cost of the contest against both the value of winning and the odds. Is the award a recognizable honor or something no one ever heard of? Are winners required to receive their awards at a conference (which they must pay to attend)? Does everyone "win"? The prize should not depend on the number of entries received and should not require additional purchases.

Contests that are free can be appealing, but take a look at the other costs that may be involved. Be particularly wary of a "free" contest that is run by a profit-making organization. As a wise person observed: if you are not the customer, you are probably the product. In other words, if there is no entry fee, the company is likely to have some other sort of financial goal. It might be gathering your email and other information to sell to marketing companies, it might be putting you on the hook to buy services or products down the line, or it might be inexpensively gaining rights to writing content that they can use or sell to others. A rule of thumb is that if it sounds too good to be true, it probably is.

Examine the contest guidelines. Any legitimate contest will post the guidelines online or make them available on request. Stay away from contests that are vague about their guidelines or make them difficult to access. Contests with excessively long and complex guidelines filled with legalese are best avoided.

How are the entries judged (are they judged at all)? Look for judging criteria, judges' names (or at least their positions), and judges' credentials. Some contests and awards programs protect the identities of their judges, but you should at least be able to determine that there *are* judges and that they have some sort of relevant expertise. Make sure that past contests have actually resulted in a published book (if that is what is promised) and that any prizes have actually been awarded. A legitimate contest organizer should be willing to supply this information.

A contest for short stories should only require you to grant onetime (or first-time) publication rights. You should still own your story. The organization running the contest will want to publish your story (and may want to be the first one to do so), but after the story appears in their publication, you should be free to publish the story in a magazine, a book, or your own anthology. Granting all rights to a short story is almost never a good idea.

Contests should never require entrants or winners to purchase books, coaching services, editing services, merchandise, or anything else. Be particularly cautious of contests held by vanity publishers and other companies that are primarily in the business of providing writing and publishing services.

Check to see what information is required to enter. You should not have to disclose anything other than basic contact information and, in some cases, writing credentials. Never provide a Social Security number, driver's license or passport information, place of birth, age, or other personal information not relevant to the contest or awards program.

The Science Fiction & Fantasy Writers of America posts comprehensive information about fake and pointless contests on the "Writer Beware" section of their website (http://www.sfwa.org/other-resources/for-authors/writer-beware/contests).

How to Submit

> Professionalism is like love: it is made up of the constant flow of little bits of proof that testify to devotion and care. Everything else is pretension or incompetence.
>
> –Tomislav Šola, *Eternity Does Not Live Here Any More—A Glossary of Museum Sins*

Submitting a story, whether to a contest or a publisher, is a business transaction. It's not a Facebook post, a shout across the fence, or a stand-up comedy gig. The manner in which you make contact, the way you address the person, and the professionalism of your materials all matter. Remember how somebody in class always asked, "Is this going to be on the test?" With submissions, it's *all* on the test.

Start by making the submission using the vehicle requested (email, postal mail, online form) and including (unless the guidelines request otherwise) some sort of polite, but brief, cover note that explains what you are submitting and what you are submitting it for (contest or publication). A line or two about your background is helpful, as long as it is pertinent (writing credentials, especially if similar publications, awards received, education). This is not the place to tell your life story or to explain that you have no writing credentials but you've "always wanted to write."

Cover notes are a courtesy but also serve an important purpose. I have received disks in the mail (with no explanation) and blank emails with a manuscript attached (often with no identifying information). These are presumably book submissions (who knows?), but I have no way of knowing whether the author has any writing credentials (doubt it), or why they are contacting me (most submissions received this way are not the kinds of things I publish). This is not the way to establish a relationship with a dentist, let alone a publisher you are hoping will be interested in publishing your work.

It will also help if your email address isn't mikeloveslisa@gmail.com, replacementwindows@hotmail.com, or myfavoritepony@

comcast.net. In other words, get yourself a professional email address. You don't need your own domain, just an email that looks businesslike. Your name, your name (if it's short) followed by "author" or "writer," or initials and a last name are some simple ways to go. Many writers maintain a separate email address for their writing so they can keep those communications separate from their personal email.

Submit a professional-looking manuscript that is as free from errors as possible. Even if no format is specified, a well-formatted manuscript puts editors, publishers, and judges in a positive frame of mind. Manuscripts that look amateurish or have obvious mistakes will distract readers from what may be a winning story.

Despite what you hear, there is no one right way to format a manuscript, although each magazine and contest has its own guidelines, and many do specify a format, so look carefully to determine the publisher's preference. If a format isn't specified, stick to a double-spaced manuscript, a common type font (Courier and Times New Roman are two popular choices), 12pt, with one-inch margins. Do not use color type and do not incorporate graphic elements unless essential to the story (a smiley face used in a character's text, for example). If mailing a hard copy, stick with standard white paper.

Unless submissions are anonymous, put your name, address, phone number, and email address in the top left corner of the first page and put the word count in the top right corner. Put the title, centered, about halfway down on the first page, followed by your author name. Use one tab indent at the beginning of each paragraph (do not space five times). And please don't think an editor, agent, or contest judge will be swayed by perfumed stationery, photographs of pets doing silly things, emoji, or stickers of unicorns and rainbows.

The "Wow Factor"

> **Write the kind of story you would like to read. If you are not writing something you like, no one else will like it either.**
>
> –Meg Cabot, "Frequently Asked Questions—On Getting Published"

Call it the "Wow Factor," "X Factor," or "That Certain Something." In contests, it's all about standing out from the crowd. Stories that take a risk, provide a sense of gravitas, or speak an emotional truth impress judges and please readers. These are not stories with distracting errors, awkward dialogue, sloppy grammar, or implausible characters. These are not clichéd romances, preachy morality plays, or predictable mysteries. The main characters are not anonymous, could-be-anyone caricatures or thinly veiled versions of the author. They are more than just polished, well-written stories. Stories that win prizes are exceptional.

Look for ways to go beyond the expected. Read the tips for any contest and you will find phrases such as "stories that break the mold," "that essential quality," and "something new." This means that to win a contest, you will want to have a memorable main character, a unique story that captivates, and a premise, situation, or setting that is unusual.

Where's the twist? Look for a way to take your premise a step in another direction. A guy decides to rob a bank—okay, but what if when he arrives he finds a bank robbery already in progress? A woman decides to break up with her boyfriend—okay, but what if he's suddenly gone missing? Keep intensifying the conflicts and you'll ramp up the appeal of your story.

Don't be afraid to be a little edgy—you want to get the judges' attention. Experiment with darkness, but most people want more than gloom and doom so try to include an element of hope or an inspirational take-away. If you have a knack for it, try humor. Readers will take more of a risk with a short story—you should too.

Be cautious with stories based on real events. Your own memories are much more interesting to you than they are to other people. Ever been a captive audience when someone described their vacation to you in nearly real time, slogging through dozens and dozens of photos while a silent scream is building in your throat? Well, keep that thought in mind when you write a story based on something that actually happened to you. Were you a government spy? Did you survive a plane crash? Were you "married to the mob"? Did you have a unique experience or at least a unique way of dealing with a common experience? If not, you may want to go a different route.

The way you tell the story is also key. Are you a terrific storyteller who can convey the emotions behind the memory and engage the reader, not just describe the memory? If so, go for it. But if your memories are more along the lines of, "I remember visiting my grandmother's house…" consider whether what you have is actually a story that people (other than your relatives) will want to read.

Also be careful with stories about the death of a loved one, surviving cancer, having a spouse with Alzheimer's, and other experiences along those lines. These are dramatic, painful events, and writing about them is cathartic for the writer, but they are also subjects that many people have written about, and unfortunately many people have been through or fear going through and may not want to read about. Unless you had an unusual way of dealing with the crisis, have specific (fresh) advice for others, or have a new approach to telling the story, you may be better off choosing a different topic.

Editor and blogger Ramona DeFelice Long (https://ramonadef.wordpress.com) interviewed several contest judges about how they choose winning stories.

"Writers seem to succeed most often when they find a way into their story that is somehow intriguing and even perhaps a little quirky," said editorial consultant and owner of Blue Horizons Communications, Laurel Marshfield. "That first sentence and first paragraph needs to set up the essence of the tale and imply that something needs resolution that is, for the moment, up in the air. How a writer does this depends upon how acutely he/she understands language—all the ways it can be used to create a fully developed world in a few thousand words. And while point of view, pacing, story arc, thematic integrity, and more are all important in creating that illusion, for me at least, the most important part is how language is shaped and molded."

Accomplished writer and experienced contest judge Mary-Margaret Pauer had this to say: "I find the first paragraph (and the last) critical in keeping the reader interested, and the story flowing. Economy of language, control of the story, use of metaphor, and character development consistent with the theme of the piece are important, and so is that exhalation of satisfaction at the end…A short story should culminate, and feel inevitable, not because the author wishes it to be so, but because character choices take the reader to the end."

"When I'm judging a short story, I'm always happy to meet interesting characters and to listen to zippy dialogue," said Dennis Lawson, who is a writer as well as the director of an arts organization. "It's also nice to jump right into a story without having to sit through a lot of setup. Some great advice I once got is that if you're going to tell a story to one of your friends, you don't say, 'Hey, I've got a great story for you, but first I'm going to tell you a bunch of background information so that you understand what's happening.' You just tell the story!"

Author and publisher Austin Camacho said, "When evaluating a short story I look first for the basics: a strong hook that draws me in and a smooth setup that leads to a satisfying payoff. A good story will make me care about at least one strong character. A *great* story will show me some character development…I'm also drawn more to a story with a clear conflict that needs to be resolved."

Voice is important to Sarah Barnett, vice president of the Rehoboth Beach Writers' Guild. "The first thing I look for in a story is a strong voice in the narrator (memoir) or main character (fiction). I wish I could describe this voice, but the best I can say is I know it when I 'hear' it. I think writers should always read their work aloud to hear how their voice is coming across and to ask themselves, 'Would I follow this person anywhere?'"

Repurposing Your Stories

> Write a short story every week. It's not possible to write 52 bad short stories in a row.
>
> –Ray Bradbury

"Repurposing" is a nice word for "recycling" or "reusing." It's a way of getting the maximum use of your story. How you repurpose your story depends on whether it was published, and if it wasn't published, whether it might be published. Even stories that are unpublishable (incomplete, flawed, or just not good enough) can sometimes be useful.

Although writers are understandably disappointed when they receive a rejection letter or learn they did not win a contest, rejection is part of the business of writing. Short stories may be rejected for many reasons that have little or nothing to do with the quality of the writing and absolutely nothing to do with the quality of the writer, so don't take it personally. Reasons for rejection include these:

- The subjectivity inherent in judging writing
- Poor match between style/content of story and targeted publication or contest
- Bad timing
- The story is too short or too long for current needs
- Publication is already complete

The wise writer examines the rejection for clues. If you are lucky, there is a stated reason for the rejection. If no reason is stated (which is much more common), you should examine the story for any flaws you can detect or ask people you trust for their ideas. If you are able to identify problem areas, look for ways to improve the story. These might include tightening up the writing, correcting any structural or grammatical errors, and looking for ways to make the story more engaging.

Once you have made any improvements you can, look for other

places to send the story. It may just have been that you didn't submit to the right place at the right time with the right piece of writing. Press on.

If your story is accepted for publication, that's wonderful, but there is no reason to stop there. Published stories can be resold (assuming you have retained the rights, which you should have). Therefore, you are free to resell published stories to other magazines, as long as you tell the magazine that the story has been previously published. You should disclose this when you submit the story, and don't waste anyone's time by submitting to publications that specifically say they don't take previously published material.

You can also submit the story to contests, although most contests will not accept previously published material. If your story was not chosen in a particular contest, you may be able to submit it to the same contest again (unless the guidelines specify otherwise). A story not selected for one contest could certainly be submitted to other contests.

You may want to publish the story as part of an anthology (your own or a multiauthor collection). Most anthologies contain works that have been previously published, so that shouldn't be a problem (again, assuming you retained the rights) and might even be an advantage, as publication provides credibility and gives you a greater chance of having the story selected for an anthology.

You may want to consider self-publishing a collection of your own stories, if you have enough for a book. If you don't have enough stories for a book, you may want to consider publishing them as Kindle Singles. The process would be similar to publishing an e-book, but the Kindle Single format is designed for shorter works.

Another way you can use story content is in blogs or as a guest blogger on someone else's blog. You will probably have to either shorten the story or serialize it. The disadvantage is that there is usually no pay or publication credit for a blog post, so unless you are using the blog to promote something else (a book, for example), this is probably not an ideal choice.

One option for a story that you just couldn't get to work is to break it apart and use parts of it in other stories. This is an ideal solution if you have a character you really liked or a scene that worked well, but the story itself never came together. Even if you don't think you will ever use the story again, don't ever delete an unfinished or unsatisfactory story, as you never know when you might revisit it and suddenly see what was wrong (and what to do about it), or find a way to scavenge its bones for bits and pieces that could fit into a different work or form the foundation for a novel.

Marketing Checklist

❐ Have you researched and identified the best potential markets for your story?

❐ Have you checked the guidelines to make sure your story is a good fit?

❐ If you are submitting to a magazine, have you examined at least three issues to check content, style, audience, and other key factors?

❐ If you are submitting to a contest, have you verified that the contest is legitimate?

❐ Have you considered anthologies?

❐ Have you looked for ways to provide the "wow factor"?

❐ Is your submission package professional, from the email address to the manuscript formatting?

❐ Have you looked for ways to repurpose your story?

BIBLIOGRAPHY

Aerogramme Writers' Studio. "Short Story Masterclasses: Eight Successful Writers Discuss the Short Story Form," August 21, 2014. http://www.aerogrammestudio.com/2014/08/21/short-story-masterclasses-eight-podcasts-thresholds.

Allen, Annie R. "Short is the New Long." *Writer's Digest*, November/December, 2014, 10-11.

Allen, Moira. "Writing Contests: When Winners Are Losers." Writing-World.com. http://www.writing-world.com/contests/scams.shtml.

Alter, Alexandra. "Her Stinging Critiques Propel Young Adult Best Sellers." *The New York Times*, April 10, 2015. http://mobile.nytimes.com/2015/04/12/business/media/the-barbed-pen-behind-the-best-sellers-of-young-adult-fiction.html?referrer&_r=3.

Bickham, Jack M. *Writing the Short Story: A Hands-On Program.* Cincinnati, OH: Writer's Digest Books, 1994.

Blood, Jen. "5 Tips for Publishing Your Own Anthology." *Novel Publicity* blog. http://www.novelpublicity.com/2012/11/5-tips-for-publishing-your-own-anthology.

Bloom, Amy. "The 'Fierce, Elegant Challenge' of Story Writing: Amy Bloom on Why Short Is Good." *Random House Reader's Circle*, December 9, 2010.

Boggess, Louise. *How to Write Short Stories That Sell.* Cincinnati, OH: Writer's Digest Books, 1980.

Brown, Jamie. *Constructing Fiction: Essays and Advice on Writing Fiction.* Milton, DE: The Broadkill Press.

Browne, Renni and Dave King. *Self-Editing for Fiction Writers.* 2nd ed. New York: HarperCollins, 2004.

Bunting, Joe. *Let's Write a Short Story*. The Write Practice, 2012.

Cabot, Meg. "Frequently Asked Questions—On Getting Published." Meg Cabot website. http://www.megcabot.com/about-meg-cabot/frequently-asked-questions-getting-published.

Clark, C. Hope. "The Red Flags of Writing Contests." *Writer Beware* blog. http://accrispin.blogspot.com/2012/08/guest-blog-post-red-flags-of-writing.html.

Copperman, Rena. "Fact (Checking) or Fiction?" Los Angeles Editors & Writers Group blog, June 20, 2012. http://laeditorsandwritersgroup.com/fact-checking-or-fiction.

Cox, Christopher. "Annie Proulx, The Art of Fiction No. 199." *The Paris Review*, Spring, 2009.

Creative Writing Now. "How to Write Short Stories from Inside Your Character's Head." *Creative Writing Now* blog. http://www.creative-writing-now.com/how-to-write-short-stories.html.

Dickson, Frank A. and Sandra Smythe, eds. *The Writer's Digest Handbook of Short Story Writing*. Cincinnati, OH: Writer's Digest Books, 1981.

Elliott, Kate. "Writing Women Characters as Human Beings." *Tor-Com* blog, March 4, 2015. http://www.tor.com/blogs/2015/03/writing-women-characters-as-human-beings.

Forge, Ashlyn. *Self-Editing On a Penny: A Comprehensive Guide*. CreateSpace Independent Publishing Platform, 2015.

Freese, Cris. "Voice in Writing: Developing a Unique Writing Voice." Writer's Digest *There Are No Rules* blog, September 12, 2013. http://www.writersdigest.com/editor-blogs/there-are-no-rules/voice-in-writing-developing-a-unique-writing-voice.

Frey, James N. *How to Write a Damn Good Novel, II*. New York: St. Martin's Press, 1994.

Galton, Della. *The Short Story Writer's Toolshed: Your Quick Read,*

Straight-To-The-Point Guide to Writing & Selling Short Fiction. Soundhaven Books, 2013.

Gilbert, Elizabeth. "The Lousy Rider." *Why I Write: Thoughts on the Craft of Fiction.* Will Blythe, ed. Boston, MA: Back Bay Books, 1999.

Hall, Sarah. *Short Story Master Class* podcast. http://blogs.chi.ac.uk/shortstoryforum/wp-content/uploads/2012/10/Short-Story-Masterclass-with-Sarah-Hall-1.mp3.

Harstone, Emily. "An Argument for Writing Short Stories." Authors Publish (online), December 11, 2014. http://www.authorspublish.com/an-argument-for-writing-short-stories.

Hart, Jack. "Building Character: What the Fiction Writers Say." *NiemanStoryboard* blog. http://niemanstoryboard.org/stories/building-character-what-the-fiction-writers-say.

Harvard University. "What's Wrong with Wikipedia?" *Harvard Guide to Using Sources.* http://isites.harvard.edu/icb/icb.do?keyword=k70847&pageid=icb.page346376.

Herron, Matt. "A Writer's Cheatsheet to Plot and Structure." *The Write Practice* blog. https://thewritepractice.com/plot-structure.

Hill, Beth. "Viewpoint Character and the Need to Choose Wisely." *The Editor's Blog*, May 26, 2011. http://theeditorsblog.net/2011/05/13/viewpoint-character-and-the-need-to-choose-wisely.

Hogrefe, Pearl. "Bringing Characters to Life." *The Writer's Digest Handbook of Short Story Writing.* Cincinnati, OH: Writer's Digest Books, 1981, p. 39.

James, Steven. "Story Trumps Structure." *Crafting Novels & Short Stories: The Complete Guide to Writing Great Fiction.* Cincinnati, OH: Writer's Digest Books, 2011, p. 74.

Jerz, Dennis G. "Short Stories: Developing Ideas for Short Fiction." *Jerz's Literacy Weblog.* http://jerz.setonhill.edu/writing/

creative1/shortstory-ideas.

Jerz, Dennis G. "Short Story Tips: 10 Ways to Improve Your Creative Writing." *Jerz's Literacy Weblog.* http://jerz.setonhill.edu/writing/creative1/shortstory.

Kardos, Michael. "How (& Where) to Get a Short Story Published." *Writer's Digest* blog, November 12, 2012. http://www.writersdigest.com/whats-new/how-where-to-get-a-short-story-published.

King, Stephen. *On Writing: A Memoir of the Craft.* New York: Scribner, 2000.

Kirwin, Faye. "How to Write Great Flash Fiction: Crafting Killer First and Last Lines." Short Story & Flash Fiction Society, May 7, 2015. http://www.shortstoryflashfictionsociety.com/how-to-write-great-flash-fiction.

Klems, Brian A. "The Difference between Voice and Style in Writing." *The Writer's Digest* blog, September 14, 2012. http://www.writersdigest.com/online-editor/the-difference-between-voice-and-style-in-writing.

Lantgen, Alexis. "Writing Short Stories." *The Wise Serpent* blog, May 1, 2015. http://thewiseserpent.blogspot.com/2015/05/writing-short-stories.html.

Lardner, Ring. *How to Write Short Stories (With Samples).* New York: Charles Scribner's Sons, 1924, republished in 1971.

Long, Ramona DeFelice. "What Do Judges & Jurors Want? Part 3 of Writing for Contests and Anthologies." Ramona DeFelice Long blog, April 23, 2015. https://ramonadef.wordpress.com/2015/04/23/what-do-judges-jurors-want-part-2-of-writing-for-contests-and-anthologies/#more-3857.

Lowenkopf, Shelly. *The Fiction Writer's Handbook.* White Whisker Books, 2012.

Lyons, Jeff. "How to Structure a Premise for Stronger Stories."

The Writer blog, September 1, 2013. http://www.writermag.com/2013/09/01/how-to-structure-a-premise-for-stronger-stories.

Maass, Donald. *Writing the Breakout Novel.* Cincinnati, OH: Writer's Digest Books, 2001.

Maddox, Maeve. "Character Tags in Fiction." *Daily Writing Tips* blog, March 25, 2009. http://www.dailywritingtips.com/character-tags-in-fiction.

Martyn, Ian. "The Power of the Short Story." Posted by Becca Puglisi, December 2, 2014. *Writers Helping Writers* blog. http://writershelpingwriters.net/2014/12/power-short-story.

Masterson, Lee. "How Long Should Your Story Be?" Writing-World.com. http://www.writing-world.com/fiction/length.shtml.

Mixon, Victoria. *The Art & Craft of Fiction: A Practitioner's Manual.* La Favorita Press, 2010.

Moore, Lorrie. "Ordinary Life Always Went Too Far." *New York Times Books*, October 22, 1989.

Nyberg, Ben. *One Great Way to Write Short Stories.* Cincinnati, OH: Writer's Digest Books, 1988.

O'Connor, Flannery. "The Nature and Aim of Fiction." *Mystery and Manners: Occasional Prose.* New York: Farrar, Straus & Giroux, 1969.

O'Connor, Flannery. "Writing Short Stories." *Mystery and Manners: Occasional Prose.* New York: Farrar, Straus & Giroux, 1969.

O'Connor, Joseph. "Advice & Inspiration for Writing Short Stories." *Dog Days & Other Stories.* Fish Publishing, 1997. http://www.fishpublishing.com/writing-short-stories.php.

O'Connor, Joseph. "Joseph O'Connor's Top 10 Tips." *Writing.ie* blog. http://www.writing.ie/resources/joseph-oconnors-top-10-tips.

Parnell, Rob. *The Easy Way to Write Short Stories That Sell.* R & R Books Film Music, 2013.

Parrish, Anne Leigh. "Mistakes to Avoid in Short Story Writing." *Women Writers, Women['s] Books* blog. http://booksbywomen.org/short-story-writing-tips-by-anne-leigh-parrish.

Patterson, Amanda. "The Four Most Important Things to Remember About Pacing." *Writers Write* blog. http://writerswrite.co.za/all-about-pacing-the-four-most-important-things-to-remember-about-pacing.

Petite, Steven. "Why Short Stories Matter." *The Huffington Post,* April 21, 2015. http://www.huffingtonpost.com/steven-petite/why-short-stories-matter-_b_7093528.html.

Power, Suzanne. "Rejection and Criticism. Advice & Inspiration for Writing Short Stories." Fish Publishing. http://www.fishpublishing.com/writing-short-stories.php.

Prunkl, Arlene. "Dialogue in Fiction: Part V—Writing Your Characters' Thoughts." PenUltimate Editorial Services blog, July 10, 2014. http://penultimateword.com/editing-blogs/dialogue-in-fiction-part-v-writing-your-characters-thoughts.

Quirk, Leslie W. *How to Write a Short Story: An Exposition of the Technique of Short Fiction.* New York: The Editor Publishing Company, 1906.

Reed, Shannon. "If Jane Austen Got Feedback From Some Guy In A Writing Workshop." *BuzzFeed Books* blog, June 10, 2015. http://www.buzzfeed.com/shannonreed/jane-austen-receives-feedback-from-tim-a-guy-in-her-mfa-work#.og1E35ymWq.

Renner, Jodie. "How to Write a Prize-Worthy Short Story: A Step-by-Step Guide." Anne R. Allen's blog, March 8, 2015. http://annerallen.blogspot.com/2015/03/how-to-write-prize-worthy-short-story.html.

Roth, Philip. *Goodbye, Columbus and Five Short Stories.* New York: Vintage Books, 1993, p. 143.

Rothstein, Mervyn. "Canada's Alice Munro Finds Excitement in Short-Story Form." *The New York Times*, November 10, 1986. http://www.nytimes.com/1986/11/10/books/canada-s-alice-munro-finds-excitement-in-short-story-form.html.

Sansevieri, Penny C. "Book Marketing Predictions for 2014." *The Huffington Post* blog, December 5, 2014. http://www.huffingtonpost.com/penny-c-sansevieri/book-marketing-prediction_b_4394295.html.

Sedwick, Helen. *Self-Publisher's Legal Handbook*. Ten Gallon Press, 2014.

Sorenson, Sharon. *How to Write Short Stories*. Lawrenceville, NJ: Thomson/Arco, 2002.

Stein, Sol. *Stein on Writing: A Master Editor of Some of the Most Successful Writers of Our Century Shares His Craft Techniques and Strategies*. New York: St. Martin's Press, 1995.

Stim, Rich. "Measuring Fair Use: The Four Factors." Stanford University Libraries, Copyright & Fair Use. http://fairuse.stanford.edu/overview/fair-use/four-factors.

Thaler, Susan. "How to Use the Flashback in Fiction." *The Writer's Digest Handbook of Short Story Writing*. Frank A. Dickson and Sandra Smythe, eds. Cincinnati, OH: Writer's Digest Books, 1981.

Vincent, Jeanne. "Theme and Premise: What's the Difference?" *Taking Notes* blog, June 14, 2007. http://www.jeannevincent.com/theme-and-premise-whats-the-difference.

Webb, Jack. "In the Beginning." *The Writer's Digest Handbook of Short Story Writing*. Frank A. Dickson and Sandra Smythe, eds. Cincinnati, OH: Writer's Digest Books, 1981.

Wendig, Chuck. "Choosing the Right Title for Your Work." *Terribleminds* blog. http://terribleminds.com/ramble/2010/04/06/choosing-the-right-title-for-your-work.

Wendig, Chuck. "In Which I Critique Your Story (That I Haven't Read)." *Terribleminds* blog. http://terribleminds.com/ramble/2015/05/05/in-which-i-critique-your-story-that-i-havent-read.

Wharton, Edith. *Edith Wharton: A Study of the Short Fiction.* New York: Twayne Publishers, 1991.

White, Barbara A. *Edith Wharton: A Study of the Short Fiction.* New York: Twayne Publishers, 1991.

Winkle, Chris. "Outline a Short Story in Seven Steps." *Mythcreants* blog. http://blog.karenwoodward.org/2015/03/a-structure-for-short-stories.html.

Writer's Digest. *Crafting Novels & Short Stories: The Complete Guide to Writing Great Fiction.* Cincinnati, OH: Writer's Digest Books, 2011.

Writer's Relief Staff. "Short Stories: Start Off With A Bang." *Writer's Relief* blog, April 13, 2008. http://writersrelief.com/blog/2008/04/short-stories-start-off-with-a-bang.

Writer's Relief Staff. "5 Ways to Shorten Your Short Stories." *Writer's Relief* blog, August 30, 2012. http://writersrelief.com/blog/2012/08/shorten-your-short-stories.

Writer's Relief Staff. "8 Techniques to Up the Drama Factor in Your Short Stories." *Writer's Relief* blog, July 18, 2014. http://writersrelief.com/blog/2014/07/drama-factor-short-stories.

Yeoman, John. "How to Write a Short Story With Deep Structure (And Win a Prize for It)." *Write to Done* blog. http://writetodone.com/win-short-story-contest-using-deep-structure.

Zipes, Jack. *The Irresistible Fairy Tale: The Cultural and Social History of a Genre.* Princeton University Press, 2012.

Index

A

B

C

Lightning Source UK Ltd.
Milton Keynes UK
UKHW022019041019
351023UK00018B/275/P

9 780986 059797